Your Dream Vacation To Italy

The most beautiful dreams are the ones that happen when your eyes are open.

© MMXXII

© MMXXII - Your Dream Vacation To Italy.
All Rights Reserved.

No portion of this book may be copied, reproduced, stored or transmitted in any form, digitally, electronically or by mechanical means, without written permission from the author.

DISCLAIMER: All companies listed in this book are current as of the date of publication (2022) and may change or close over time. The author has not received sponsorship from any of the websites and businesses mentioned.

The 1st thing to pack for your dream vacation is your dreams themselves, which will become realities that will transform into memories, the most precious "souvenir" you'll take home.

Money spent to purchase your special trip is like making an investment in yourself with a guarantee return far more precious than the amount you put in, on "things" that can't be bought:
the awe of standing before a monument that has stood there for thousands of years as the world changes; the thrill of a breathtaking view suddenly unfolding before your eyes; the irresistible aroma of freshly baked pastries from a bakery down an alley captivating your senses as you walk by;
above all,
the inner joy of living in the moment you've long dreamed of.

Your 1st trip to Italy marks the beginning of many other trips you'll want to take in your life...leading you back to Italy.

An Italian proverb:
"Chi vive vede molto, chi viaggia vede di piu'".
Those who live see a lot, those who travel see more.

Contents:

Chapter	Page
1) A dream vacation to Italy	5
2) Three main cities you cannot miss (especially if this is your 1st trip)	7
3) Cities and towns totally worth visiting	26
4) Tuscany	56
5) Seaside places	59
6) Mountains and Lakes	77
7) Best ways to travel Italy and get the most out of it	93
8) Italy on a budget	98
9) Food (and my favorite places to eat when I am in Rome)	102
10) A few more words….	115
11) Your travel notes	117

A DREAM VACATION TO ITALY

"Ohhh you are from Italy! I always wanted to go to Italy! And where in Italy?"

"Rome."

"Rome? Rome is my favorite city in the entire world!!"

This conversation was happening all the time in the store where I worked right after moving to America in 2006. Upon hearing my foreign accent, customers would always ask me "Where are you from?" From that point on, they would completely forget they were in a store looking for clothes. All they wanted to talk about was when they went to Italy and visited so many beautiful places, what I would recommend them to see in Rome, or where they should go besides visiting the three most famous cities in Italy: Rome, Florence and Venice. Others who had never been to Italy were looking for suggestions for planning their trip.

I have always enjoyed giving travel tips to customers who would ask me all sorts of questions about a trip to Italy. My manager, however, was less thrilled, she wanted me to sell, sell, sell, not talk, talk, talk. I remember one time she wrote on a sheet of paper in big bold capital letters "SELL!!!" and held it with her arms raised above her head for me to see when the customers were not looking. I must admit it was hilarious! She was a good manager with a sense of humor, sales goal oriented 110% of the time. Ok, I am getting sidetracked here, let's get back to the main subject.

Year after year, Italy is always one of the most visited countries in the world: with its many facets to enjoy, people from all over and with the most diverse cultures, find what their heart desires when they visit it. There really is something (indeed a lot!) for everyone. The beauty, charm, wealth of history, art, culture, and nature that Italy has to offer are truly innumerable. When I go back to Italy to visit family and friends, I enjoy every small or big city and landscape, with fresh eyes like a tourist who sees and admires something beautiful for the first time, but with the knowledge of a local.

After years of sharing suggestions on what to see or do in Italy, I thought I would write a book on destinations to visit, as well as tips, ideas and how-to, from the perspective of an experienced native traveler who turned her passion for travel into a profession. In Italy, where I completed my studies, I took a 3-year course to become a travel consultant, planning travel itineraries, excursions, tours, cruises and other activities.

Travelling is discovery, fun, sometimes an unforgettable, life-enriching experience, and your next trip to Italy could be too! It is a unique country in many ways, starting with its very particular shape, a long boot (my favorite type, the high-heeled one!).

A vacation in Italy can take so many different paths. What do you look for when you travel? Culture, history, arts, amazing landscapes like mountain peaks, or relaxing on a pristine beach, perhaps a mix of all of the above? There is such a variety of places to see, things to do and experience that a visitor would wish to stay for 2 months!

The purpose of this book is to give you an overall idea (in some cases with little-known side stories, legends and curiosities) of amazing places and hidden gems to visit in terms of historical and architectural sites, this is usually the main reason for a trip to Italy, as well as its spectacular seascapes and landscapes across the country. In between tours, you want to enjoy something else that Italy is world famous for: its extraordinary cuisine! We can't skip or skimp on this mouthwatering topic, can we? As they say, keep your fork, as the delicious chapter on Italian food will go into detail.

I will also share practical tips to help you make the best decision on how to spend and make the most of your vacation according to your wishes and tastes. Starting with the places and things you found and liked most in this book and your own ideas, to choose what to see and do, based on the length of your stay. Taking some time to prepare your trip will help you make the best of it once there. By the end of this book, you will look forward to visiting Italy even more, you'll start looking for plane tickets!

"All roads lead to Rome", so get ready, your journey, your road to Rome and Italy, is already starting here and now through this book taking you to places that will fill your imagination and dreams until you are there to live…. Your Dream Vacation To Italy!

I am going to tell you about:

- **THREE MAIN CITIES YOU CANNOT MISS (especially if this is your 1st trip)**
- **CITIES AND TOWNS TOTALLY WORTH VISITING**
- **TUSCANY**
- **SEASIDE PLACES**
- **MOUNTAINS AND LAKES**
- **BEST WAYS TO TRAVEL THE COUNTRY AND GET THE MOST OUT OF IT**
- **ITALY ON A BUDGET**
- **FOOD** (and my favorite places to eat when I am in Rome)

Let's start Your Dream Vacation To Italy!

THREE MAIN CITIES

If you only have a week to explore and especially if this is your 1st time in Italy, I suggest you spend it in Rome, Florence, and Venice. Each one of them is overwhelmingly rich with historical sights, amazing in beauty and unique in different ways.

Roma
Exploring Rome to the fullest could easily take up a week or more, given the incredible number of historical points of interest, archeological sites and monuments all over the city.
To give you an idea of how many archeological finds there are in Rome, just imagine that you can even find some at the Ikea store in the southern side of Rome, Anagnina area. In case you were wondering, no, they are not part of their sales! There is an exhibit in the main entrance. The reason is that when they started excavating to build the foundation for the store, many artifacts dated about 2000 years were discovered and unburied. It was decided to have them showcased right at the location where they were found and brought to light again.
You can see at least the main sights and even include a couple of museums in 3 full days. One nice thing about the Eternal City is that most of Rome's famous landmarks are all more or less in the same area, so all you have to do is put on some comfortable shoes and walk around. No matter where your hotel is, downtown Rome is well connected with many bus lines and an efficient subway system. A great place to start might be from Piazzale Flaminio.
If you take the Metro Linea A (Line A) get off at Flaminio, walk to Piazza del Popolo and from there to Via Del Corso, Rome's most famous street full of shops, street food eateries and bars (in Italy a bar is not the same as a bar in the USA or the UK. Quite the opposite. It is more like a café' where they mostly sell yes, the famous caffe' espresso, panini, gelati, cappuccino and pastries).

Along the way to so many incredible historical sites you can also enjoy the "sightseeing" of the latest fashion trends from the many shops in the area.
If you are more in the mood for some high-end fashion statements, and to you Italy also means being a glamourous fashionista, then you will have your eyes filled just minutes away. Halfway through via del Corso turn left into posh via Condotti, where the most iconic Italian designers such as Valentino, Dolce &

Gabbana, and Giorgio Armani among others, have their prestigious boutiques, and you will certainly find what your heart desires. Via Condotti is the place where the seduction and elegance of fashion literally meet with the seduction and elegance of history combined with art.
There you are, in Piazza di Spagna. One of the most well-known squares in the world, made famous by its iconic landmarks, Barcaccia Fountain, and the Spanish Steps. The Barcaccia fountain has the shape of a half sunken boat (barca in Italian) with water flowing into it. The legend says that in 1598 the Tiber River flooded, and a small boat was carried into the square. When the waters receded, the boat was found in the center of the square. Sculptor and architect Bernini was so inspired by the sunken boat that years later, in 1629, a baroque style sculpture of a boat, La Barcaccia, was completed.

Stop for a moment and look at the scene: you have just arrived in Piazza di Spagna, with the Barcaccia and the Spanish Steps opening before your eyes! What a view…. from the bottom up! As you embrace this moment, you approach the steps. You have a smile on your face as you think: "I am here in Rome!". Yes, you are! While you are still looking at it, you enthusiastically begin to climb the 300 years old staircase (built in 1725) to the top. After 138 easy steps and reaching the top, Trinita' dei Monti, you will be rewarded with an even better view waiting for you to enjoy, the view…. from top to bottom!

Look all around at all the details, the roofs, the restaurant with the terrace overlooking the square, the elegant street where you just came from, via Condotti, the horse-drawn carriages, the people strolling around. Now all you can think about is taking the best shots to save this unforgettable moment not only in your memory but also in the memory card of your camera. Go ahead, take lots of pictures.
From that point overlooking the square you have 2 choices: an easy 10-minute walk to Pincio Hill, where you can enjoy another amazing view, and stroll in the beautiful Villa Borghese, the "Central Park" of Rome, with small pretty lakes, museums, and cafes; or walk in the opposite direction, (you can still go to Villa Borghese another time) to the most famous fountain in Rome: la Fontana di Trevi. This Fountain is a grandiose monument from the Baroque era, in my opinion a truly majestic masterpiece (in case you were wondering what my favorite monument is, yes, it is the Trevi Fountain). So many details and meanings behind the beautifully carved stonework's and what they symbolize. So much drama in it! Just to give you an idea of what is represented in the center, the main statue in the middle of the Fountain represents Oceanus, the other two are Abundance and Health. Oceanus and his chariot

are pulled by two sea horses. One is wild and the other is docile, they represent the ever-changing mood of the sea. Speaking of mood, if you have the time, visit the Trevi Fountain both during the day and at night. The night lighting makes it even more fascinating and gives a different mood to the impressive monument and the area itself.
By the way, the most iconic scene in the famous film "La Dolce Vita" by director Federico Fellini was shot in that fountain, but do not t try to imitate it, unless you want to have, among other souvenirs, a very expensive ticket from the Italian police that always surrounds the area.

From the Trevi Fountain, you could walk back to Via del Corso towards piazza Venezia. On the way there, and again speaking of mood, if you are still in a shopping mood, you could head to Via del Tritone. Along the way you can find La Rinascente, a high-end contemporary department store that caters only to the highest quality and chic couture fashion brands, beautiful to see even from the escalator. Returning to Via del Corso, right on the corner, inside a historic building surrounded by columns, is the Galleria Alberto Sordi, named after the Italian actor Alberto Sordi. It was formerly called Galleria Colonna because it is in front of the large Piazza Colonna. This elegant indoor shopping center was built in the early 1900s and has beautiful cafes, restaurants and shops.

At the end of Via del Corso, you will see Piazza Venezia, a very large, busy square and an intersection with the Altare della Patria (Altar of the Fatherland) building, standing in the middle. The Altare della Patria is a white, imposing monument to commemorate the Unknown Soldier.
There is a museum inside and, at the top of the building, also a beautiful terrace with an elegant bar and outdoor seating, perfect to enjoy some light meals or desserts while looking out over the large, crowded square down below or on the other side of the terrace, where you can peek out and see... the Colosseum! Enjoying a good caffe' espresso from the top of the Altare della Patria with the view of the square below, the Colosseum in the distance, is one of the many nice things to take the time to do while visiting the city.
I mentioned the Colosseum, which is practically a stone's throw from Piazza Venezia, so let's keep walking towards it. Not only is the walk very pleasant because it is a beautiful, very large pedestrian street, but historically speaking, it is extremely engaging and fascinating.
Via dei Fori Imperiali (the Roman Forum, or in Latin, Forum Romanum, as the ancient Romans called it 2000 years ago) is home to an incredible site. Just looking at it will make you feel like you are 2000 years back in time. With a little imagination as you walk down on the cobblestone street, you might even

visualize what life was like back then by looking at the buildings on the left side and all the tall columns on the right side.
The ruins that are still visible can give you an idea of how important the forum was in the life of the Romans of that time, as all the crucial events took place there. The Roman Forum was the place where public meetings and court speeches were held, where locals went to shop in the open-air markets and where gladiators could be seen fighting in the nearby Colosseum.

An impressive, overwhelming and beautiful place that I never tire of visiting or simply passing by, despite having been there countless times, living in Rome most of my life. When I walk down via Fori Imperiali, I still find something new to see or a little new detail of history to photograph. Truly an amazing place. As you approach the Colosseum, it is also noteworthy to stop and look at the huge marble stones (on the right side of the street) that depict to what extent far and wide the mighty Roman Empire expanded. Who knows, maybe you might have Roman roots too, hello fellow Roman!

Then, there it is, in front of you: THE COLOSSEUM! One of the most famous monuments in the world, arguably the number one and most impressive structure a tourist might want to see in Rome, il Colosseo, (originally named Amphitheater Flavio in honor of emperor Flavio) lives up to its name and fame. With more than 2000 years of history, this ancient amphitheater still makes a striking impression standing tall with its mighty presence and is still the largest in the world. It could hold up to 80,000 spectators. It was used for entertainment (from athletic competitions, chariot races, theatrical shows by mimes, to ruthless animal or gladiator fights) until the beginning Medieval era. The construction itself makes it truly a one-of-a-kind architectural and historical masterpiece, with few other smaller versions elsewhere in the Old Continent. The nearby Arco di Tito (Arch of Titus) built in 81 AD, is a triumphal arch in honor of Emperor Titus, and depicts in its upper part the victory of the army in Jerusalem.

As with the Trevi Fountain, I recommend visiting the Colosseum and the Arch during the day for better sightseeing, and in the evening when the lights surrounding these imposing structures make them more suggestive.
Since we are still in the Colosseum area, I will suggest something. I am not a big fan of touristy restaurants near monument sites, but just this once I'll make an exception. Look for a restaurant near the Colosseum along the cobbled main street, choose an entrée such as a thin-crusted Roman pizza, or a delicious local dish like pasta alla carbonara, or the famous risotto alla crema

di scampi (throwing out ideas on some of my favorite Roman dishes), and while you are sitting enjoying your appetizing meal, glimpse at the view of the Colosseum and Via dei Fori Imperiali. What a superlative area, full of character with a world masterpiece that is over 2000 years old! You are just eating and looking, but it is almost as you can sense all the history that happened on these streets thousands of years ago.
After your tasty Roman meal with a view, if you feel it's time to head back to the hotel, there is a subway adjacent to the Colosseum, or you can also turn around and walk in the opposite direction, back to Piazzale Flaminio, because when we started this tour from Piazzale Flaminio going to Via del Corso, Piazza di Spagna etc, I only mentioned the monuments on the left side of Via del Corso, but there are also incredible sites on the right side!
Going back, on the left side of the street, just before the Altare della Patria, you can see a small climb that leads to the Campidoglio, the Capitoline Hill, another beautiful site rich in history also with museums to visit. (As a side note, civil marriages for residents of Rome are celebrated at the Campidoglio)

I like to wander the side streets. Not only is it fun, but it also feels like going on a treasure hunt, where the "treasure" is finding that beautiful square that suddenly appears in front of you, like Piazza Navona for example.
Arriving at piazza Navona after walking through the narrow streets (there are many signs directing you to the square, do not worry about getting lost) full of crowded restaurants, gelaterie, people walking at all hours, is amusing, as I walk, I look around, glance at the menu signs hanging on the front door of restaurants or peek inside the shops. The moment I enter the square, the view is as stunning as ever. I stop, look, and think: "wow!" I love Piazza Navona.

There are many things that make this long oval square so charming. It is another great example of Baroque style architecture at its best. There are three impressive fountains, the largest being the one that everybody flocks to, with its imposing presence and the loud rushing of the waters, called La Fontana dei Quattro Fiumi (Fountain of the Four Rivers) with the large and tall Roman obelisk in the center. The fountain depicts four rivers: the Ganges, the Nile, the Danube, and the Rio de la Plata. The four rivers and the four large figures next to them represent the four continents known at the time (Oceania was not yet known to Europeans at the time). The fountain was built in 1651 .by Lorenzo Bernini. The church Sant'Agnese in Agona, which overlooks the Fountain of four Rivers was designed by Borromini.
The square is surrounded by charming old residences all on top of each other, overlooking the stunning and very entertaining scenes happening below.

Many restaurants, cafes, and stalls selling mostly landscapes paintings, streets performers and musicians, all contribute to the delightful atmosphere that makes every evening passeggiata (stroll) so pleasant. The square hosts outdoor fairs and markets. Not far from Piazza Navona, there is another famous piazza where locals love to hang out at night, Piazza Campo de Fiori. This lively square, although much smaller than piazza Navona, is also famous for its open-air market.

Close to Campo de Fiori, is Piazza della Rotonda, what makes this square world- famous is the impressive building in it: The Pantheon. This Roman temple was built around 120 A.D. Even though it is almost 2000 years old, it is incredibly well preserved and has weathered the storms that have taken place during this very, very long time. And when I say storms, I mean literal ones. The building has an impressive dome, the largest brick dome in the world, with a 9 meters (about 30 feet) hole in the center. As you can imagine, lots of rain fell inside over these nearly 2000 years, but because the floor is slightly convex, the water flows away and dries out quickly.

The church has no windows, so the huge ceiling-hole is the only way for the church to have some light. When looking at it, it is baffling to think how they came up with the concept and managed to build it. At that time even the simplest scaffolding techniques did not exist, but nevertheless that very challenging task of building the dome with the opening in the middle was achieved and we still marvel at it today, 2000 years later.

Visiting these three squares and the surrounding areas with their fascinating little alleys full of restaurants and shops bustling until the late hours of the night, will keep you busy and entertained even if you just stroll around. So, get out and have fun!

Vatican City: The country within the country, with the city within the city. The city of Rome has a foreign state and city within itself. The smallest state in the world, the Vatican has a population of less than 1000 inhabitants, is not open to tourism and therefore cannot be visited by anyone. Not even Romans who live just outside its walls can enter. Of course, this does not apply to the very impressive Basilica di San Pietro, St. Peter Basilica, an outstanding work of art from the Renaissance era.

To give you a quick idea of this construction from an architectural standpoint, think of its ceiling: very high all over, with a dome reaching its highest point, 120 meters (394 feet), built about 500 years ago, without any of the technology we have nowadays. Now think of all the paintings and frescos that cover every inch of the ceiling. To paint such high ceiling, being attentive to the smallest detail of each fresco, imagine what difficult working conditions Michelangelo had to endure (my neck hurts just thinking about it). Of course, his assistants and other artists contributed to the result, but Michelangelo, being also an architect, was behind most of the projects in the Basilica until his death. He certainly was one the most talented artist and sculptor of all times.

The visit to the St. Basilica is free for the most part, but the line at the entrance can last hours. Plan your visit accordingly. Also, keep in mind the dress code to enter: no shorts or skirts above the knee, and no sleeveless or lowcut shirts.

Just a few minutes walking distance from the Vatican on the Tiber River, right in the center of Rome, stands a castle with its imposing presence: Castel Sant'Angelo. With its large walls, this cylindrical shape fort built in the 1st century A.D. is another must-see stop on your tour of Rome. It was built as a mausoleum and burial place for Roman emperors. During the Middle Ages it was also used as a place of refuge especially for the popes, who could escape through a long tunnel that connected the Lateran residence to the castle.

Castel Sant'Angelo is another example of a monument that should be visited both during the day, (it is a very interesting museum to visit, with an internal courtyard, apartments, prison cells and amazing views from the top floor for great pictures) and at night, especially during the summer months when the whole area becomes extra lively with artisans' stalls selling anything from souvenirs, clothes and books to delicious street food.

Near the castle if you are in for a night at the movies, they show "movies under the stars", or if you would like to listen to some music, you can enjoy street performers singing and playing. So pleasant to walk around the area, and although I have been there often over the years, I still sometimes find myself photographing the Tiber River, the castle or the bridge from different angles to capture in my camera not only the sites, but also that beautiful atmosphere.

By the way, have you ever seen the movie Roman Holiday, starring the lovely actress Audrey Hepburn and Gregory Peck? The movie was filmed in Rome and shows many famous locations and landmarks. Castel Sant'Angelo is one of them (if you have never seen this 1950s romantic comedy, take the time to do so, it is a beautiful classic and, if you are planning a Roman holiday, you might start by watching Roman Holiday, you will also want to ride a Vespa afterwards!). Holiday goes hand in hand with hotel. My favorite hotel in Rome is Hotel Rocco Forte de Russie, in via del Babbuino 9. Absolutely sumptuous. This 5-star luxurious hotel and its interior garden exude elegance at its finest.

We just took a tour of the main and most famous historical landmarks in Rome. If you wander around the Eternal City, you will come across countless other sites, monuments, fountains, arches, city walls, and ancient ruins, which testify how much history is carved in this city. New sites come to light, such as the imposing Mausoleum of emperor Augustus dated to 28 BC, after extensive excavations opened its doors to the public in 2021, located near via del Corso. A must see. As I said, you will live, breathe and feel the history everywhere, learn interesting stories about who built what and why, and side curiosities on this or that. Just as an example, I was walking from Piazzale Flaminio towards the main train station, stazione Termini, which I had done many times. Arriving in Piazza della Repubblica, which is very close to the train station, I realized that I was quite early, so I decided to take a walk around the square and the massive Bagni di Diocleziano. This structure was built from 298 to 306 AD. It is so large and widespread that I was surprised and amused at the same time by the fact it took "only" 8 years to build. I thought to myself "Wow, the ancient Romans must have had a much better organized bureaucracy than the modern Romans!" Nowadays it can take a long time to get building permits. But what surprised even more was the small sign I read at the entrance to I Bagni di Diocleziano (The Baths of Diocletian), which stated that these baths could accommodate more than 3000 people at once. I had no idea they were that vast, and that is what I am referring to regarding side curiosities. There is always something new to learn in a city as large, ancient and historic as Rome.

An area I love, along with many fellow Romans, is Trastevere. This is another historic neighborhood. The name Trastevere comes from a Latin word meaning "beyond Tiber", which is the river that crosses and divides the city. The charming old quarter of Trastevere is the true heart of Rome and much loved by Romans and tourists who discover it, in these narrow-cobbled streets and alleys you can find a lot of history and art. One of these is the church of Santa Maria in Trastevere, where upon entering you can appreciate its gold mosaics from the 13th century.

Not only history in the area. Filled with many pubs, small typical Roman restaurants, shops open till very late at night, Trastevere is another perfect place to hang out and spend a lovely and lively night out. Finding a parking space there at night, particularly on weekends can be challenging, often unlikely. Sometimes it is better to take a taxi or public transport instead of wasting the evening looking for parking especially if, being on vacation, you are in Rome for a short time and you want to make the most of it.

Right across from Trastevere, right in the middle of the Tiber River, there is the Isola Tiberina (Tiberina Island). Correct, there is an island in Rome!

The small island can be accessed through the two short bridges that connect its two sides. The name Tiberina derives from the Latin word Tiberis, which today is called Tevere in Italian (Tiber in English); therefore, Isola Tiberina is the Island of Tiber (and this was the Latin-Italian-English lesson of the day). The island is mainly known for three things:

1: Ristorante Sora Lella. A famous restaurant that for decades has been serving truly authentic, typical Roman dishes and delicacies. It is located in the center of the island, next to the only square on the only short road between the two bridges, you can't miss it.

2: Roman summer on the island. From the end of June to the end of August, the island entertains its visitors on summer nights with movies under the stars, live music, dancing, outdoor lounges, craft booths and street food to name a few. Definitely a fun way to spend an evening out on summer nights (and you can tell your friends you even went dancing on an island one night!)

3: Fatebenefratelli hospital. Yes, the world's smallest inhabited island has made room on its very limited soil for a hospital. Hey, life is all about priorities..

From Isola Tiberina (and from other areas) you can take a boat on the river for a romantic cruise dinner, or during the day for the hop and off sightseeing tour and excursions. Info on www.turismoroma.it (type -Rome by boat- on the search bar).

As soon as you leave Isola Tiberina, if you continue for a little over 1 mile and then turn left on Ponte Sublicio, you will arrive in Testaccio, an old working-class neighborhood, interesting and full of contrasts. The Monte Testaccio district is known for the Monte dei Cocci, a place where there are innumerable pieces and fragments of ancient Roman broken pottery, in terracotta or earthenware, dating back to the time of the Roman Empire. These cocci (shards) accumulated so much over time that they became a small mountain about 150 feet high. Today in the Roman dialect the word cocci refers to something that accidentally breaks into pieces, the cocci are what is left of it. Testaccio district was also known for a very large slaughterhouse, its many taverns and night clubs always very noisy. In recent years some of these places have been gentrified, for example the slaughterhouse has become a nice covered market, Mercato Testaccio.

Testaccio is most famous for two monuments in the area, which are still there solid and strong for about 2000 years. The imposing Porta San Paolo, built in the third century AD on commission of the emperor Aurelio, was the southernmost gate of the Aurelian walls to enter the city of Rome.

Porta San Paolo is not just a gate; it can also be visited since it has become a museum. The other monument very close to Porta San Paolo is a pyramid. Yes you read it correctly. Who would have ever thought to arrive in Rome and find a pyramid in the center of the city? In Rome we also have a pyramid, much smaller than the Egyptian ones, but certainly impressive. But why is there a pyramid in Rome? The story is quite curious.

The Piramide Cestia is a funeral monument dedicated to Gaius Cestius Epulone, a powerful man of ancient Rome. He wanted to have a pyramid built in the fashion of those times, as Egypt had just been conquered by Emperor Augustus in 30 BC. Gaius Cestius ordered his heirs to build this funeral monument within 330 days of his death, under penalty of loss of the inheritance. Well, the heirs were very eager to complete this "monumental task" (these 2 words could not be more accurate, literally) in time to inherit the will. And so it was, in fact, the Latin inscription the heirs left above the monument says it was completed a few days early, so everyone knew that it had been built within the time frame. Just as the old saying goes, "where there is a ...will, there is a way"!

You may be wondering if there is a place in Rome from which you can enjoy a beautiful view of the city from above, the answer is si, yes. Two places with spectacular views of Rome are the Belvedere del Gianicolo and the Zodiaco. The Gianicolo is an area where there is also a big park with trees and paths to walk or bike not far from Trastevere and reachable by bus. A peculiarity and tradition of this park well known by the Romans that attracts many tourists, is the cannon of the Gianicolo, which has been firing every day at noon for centuries. The Zodiaco is in the Monte Mario area, from the last bus stop you can walk uphill or take a cab. Amazing views that expand far into the distance. A less touristy, intriguing area to visit is Coppede in the Trieste district, with slightly eccentric looking buildings in Liberty, Deco style and a hint of Baroque.

If you want to do other ctivities besides sightseeing, there is no shortage of choices In Rome. Cultural ones like museums? Galleria Borghese, adjacent to Villa Borghese Park is one of my favorites, Palazzo Barberini, a Baroque palace with art gallery, the Doria Pamphili Galleriy, so elegant and opulent, Villa Farnesina, a Reinassance villa with art gallery and frescos, the nearby Galleria Corsini, a Baroque place and art gallery, just to name a few.

Perhaps you are interested in visiting the Palace where the Italian President carries out his institutional and official functions. You can book a visit to the Palazzo del Quirinale online (preferably well in advance). The website is www.palazzo.quirinale.it Rome has a wide selection of different types of museums, you can spend weeks visiting them and always be fascinated by it. Choose the one that best suits the mood of the moment from history to art, you can also choose the era that most interests you, Roman, Medieval, Gothic, Renaissance, Baroque or Modern. At the Musei Capitolini you can find all of that in a matter of a few clicks. www.museicapitolini.org By the way, Musei Capitolini are the oldest museum in the world. Founded in the 14th century.

A museum where you could start your tour of Rome even before you start visiting the actual sites, is the Welcome to Rome Museum. Learn about the history of Rome in an engaging, interactive way, and the kids will love it! www.welcometo-rome.it How about living like an ancient Roman for a day? When in Rome do as .. the ancient Romans did! Dress, eat, ride a chariot and much more. A theme park for the whole family. www.RomaWorld.it

If you are looking for a museum with no historical or archeological importance, something you can easily recognize without an audio guide, look no further: the Wax Museum near Piazza Venezia will keep you amusingly entertained! Malls, parks where you can rent scooters or bikes, amusement parks, cinemas in English, a beautiful zoo, the list is endless. If you like flea markets, a huge, crowded one, is Porta Portese just past Trastevere, every Sunday morning.

Are you particularly passionate about food? You have certainly come to the most famous country in the world for its cuisine. From sophisticated taste and palate to earthy food, to slow food, street food, new trends and everything in between, there is no shortage of places to find what your heart (and belly) desires as you walk and make your own "discoveries" or read about them first. I will go into more detail about what-and-where in Rome in the FOOD chapter. By the way, the oldest restaurant in Rome is La Campana opened its doors in 1518, while at the Costanza Hostaria you can enjoy a fine meal inside a special setting: sitting next to the walls and ruins of a 2000 years old Roman theater!

There is much more to Rome than what I have described. A city so ancient and historical, you will find artifacts, monuments, statues, mausoleums, just by walking around. Largo Argentina for example. In this beautiful square where Julius Caesar was stabbed to death over 2000 years ago, you can still see the ancient ruins of that time and get an idea of what it was like then. You will also see fountains. Rome is the city of fountains. Besides the artistic ones, the ones you can drink from or fill (I do) your empty water bottle. They are everywhere. Geographically, Rome is in an excellent position. Centrally located in the Lazio region, Rome is 45 minutes from the sea and its many coastal towns, 40 minutes from Lake Bracciano with its pretty towns of Anguillara, Bracciano and Trevignano. Only an hour to Mount Terminillo for those who enjoy long hikes or skiing. Cute country villages like Frascati and Ariccia (known for its signature street food panino with porchetta and local wine) are also close to Rome. Yes, thanks to its position it makes it easy convenient for both locals and visitors to be able to go to so many different places in a short amount of time.

One more thing about Rome. A vacation in Rome is not complete without a visit to Villa D'Este, an enchanting place in Tivoli, a town about 35 miles from Rome. Built in 1550, with its stunning Italian Renaissance gardens, 500 splendid fountains, water organ fountain (not to be missed it when it plays), ornamental monuments, statues and pools, Villa D'Este is one of the finest examples of Renaissance architecture and a UNESCO World Heritage. As you listen to the pleasant sound of the waters, you will enjoy walking around, wanting to take perfect photos to capture the idyllic moments that will last forever. Speaking of sound of waters, just a short walk from Villa D'Este is Parco Villa Gregoriana, a park with ancient Roman temples, caves and the roaring Aniene waterfalls.

As Rome is the capital and largest city in Italy with an incredible amount of history and art, the city where I was born and lived most of my life, I took a little more time to describe the key points about it in more detail. The upcoming cities will be reviewed at a slightly faster speed.
Buckle up and let's go!

Firenze

Florence is about 3 hours north of Rome by car and half the time if you go by fast train. It is a much smaller city than Rome, which makes it easier to visit just by walking around the historic center. However, Florence is a city incredibly rich in history and art. Priceless sculptures and paintings by artists such as Michelangelo, Giotto, Raffaello, Caravaggio and Leonardo Da Vinci, just to name a few, can be seen in a handful of places in the historic center of this fascinating city.
The three most famous buildings, the Cathedral Santa Maria del Fiore, which is the fourth largest Cathedral in Europe (after St. Peter Basilica in Rome, St. Paul church in London and the Duomo in Milan), Santa Maria Novella Basilica and il Museo di Palazzo Vecchio (Old Palace Museum) in the famous piazza della Signoria, are just few blocks away from each other and very suggestive in sight. The Cathedral of Santa Maria del Fiore, with its cupola overlooking all the other surrounding buildings of the city, is the most iconic landmark of Florence. Rightly so.
Upon arriving at the site, one can only marvel at its impressive size. The cathedral stands mighty and majestic, you approach it, you begin to look at the gothic style décor of the façade, the minute details it contains, the green, pink and white marble panels, it truly gives a unique look to the Duomo. Construction began in 1298 AD, then in 1436 AD the esteemed architect and artist Filippo Brunelleschi completed the dome, or cupola.

The Basilica of Santa Maria Novella, one of the major churches in Florence, began to come to light in 1279 and completed centuries later as the Duomo Santa Maria del Fiore. The nearby main train station, Santa Maria Novella, takes its name from the church.

In piazza della Signoria, the largest and most famous piazza (square) in Florence, is where Palazzo Vecchio was built. This massive medieval fortress, built in the 13th century, is the seat of the city's government and a museum. In some architectural parts of Palazzo Vecchio there is also the great medieval poet, Dante Alighieri, the author of the epic poem Divina Commedia (Divine Comedy). One part is called "Guelph" and the other "Ghibelline", referring to the historical and political conflict between these two parties at that time. The building features courtyards, large halls, and a ceiling decorated with frescoes.

At the main entrance of Palazzo Vecchio, stands the world-famous statue, the David of Michelangelo. This sculpture is not the original but a replica of it. The Renaissance masterpiece, in 1873, well over 350 years after being outside in the Piazza where you can now see its replica, was moved to its current location at the Galleria dell'Accademia to be better preserved from damage.

Literally a two-minute walk from Palazzo Vecchio going towards the Arno River, there is one of the most, if not the most, famous and prominent art museum in Italy: la Galleria degli Uffizi, the Uffizi Gallery. The gallery is one of the oldest, most beautiful and best-known museums in the world and houses the largest collection of priceless masterpieces from the Middle Ages to the Renaissance. Wonderful sculptures and paintings in a stunning architectural setting that can only enhance the beauty of each piece. Paintings such as la Venere di Botticelli (the Birth of Venus) to Caravaggio, Giotto, or Leonardo da Vinci, are all exhibited at the Uffizi.

Of course, you can find more contemporary museums as well. The Uffizi Gallery is one of the most popular tourist destinations in Florence, and while is not necessary to book in advance, I highly recommend doing so. A couple of times in the past, I have been to Florence and because of the almost day-long line at the entrance, I could not get in to visit it. Here is the website to make reservations: www.uffizi.it

The Uffizi is not the only art gallery in Florence: Palazzo Pitti, (Pitti Palace) is another grand example of the encounter between history and art. The word grand is very appropriate to describe this building: massive! It was built in 1440 and has an austere appearance on the outside, but rich and elegant in the interior walls, corridors, and galleries. It was the residence of the Medici family, a very influential banking family who ruled Florence during the Renaissance period. They used their influence to beautify the arts and humanisms in Florence, which became a very important cultural city in Europe as early as the 15th century. You have probably heard the name of the best-known member of the family, Lorenzo de' Medici, also called Lorenzo il Magnifico (Lorenzo the Magnificent).

Centuries later, Pitti Palace was the residence of two royal dynasties: The Habsburg and the Savoia. Furthermore, the Bonaparte family lived there for a few years. Ah, if these walls could talk, we could hear some very interesting stories that have marked history!

Pitti Palace is the largest museum in Florence, housing paintings by Raffaello, Tiziano, Tintoretto, Caravaggio and other excellent names in art. Behind Pitti Palace is the wonderful Giardino di Boboli (Boboli Garden), the historic park of the city of Florence. The De Medici family created the layout of the beautiful gardens, adding great beauty to the area to this day. Among other things, there is a grotto, a small amphitheater and an outdoor museum with a large collection of statues that complement the beautiful surrounding architecture. It is possible to book a tour of Palazzo Pitti or Giardino di Boboli from the same Uffizi website.

From the Uffizi, looking towards the Arno River, turn right and in a few steps, you will be at the Ponte Vecchio. One of my favorite places to visit and stroll around, and its history is quite interesting too. This glorious bridge, which is not just a bridge, but a collection of buildings attached to each other, was the only one of the 6 bridges spared by the Germans when they retreated in 1944 during World War II. When it was built in 1345 AD it was full of butcher's shop, so as you can imagine, the lack of a refrigeration system at the time, caused a very unpleasant smell (to say the least) in the area, until Grand Duke Fernandino issued an edict to convert the butcher shops into goldsmiths and today it is full of jewelers and leather goods stores. Quite a change, isn't it?

Florence is very famous for its pure Italian leather artifacts, and you can find them there in all forms, leather jackets, bags, purses and accessories. If you are planning to buy leather goods during your trip in Italy, Florence is one of the best places to go.

From Ponte Vecchio you can take a small walk uphill to the giardino Bardini, a beautiful garden with many fountains, different kinds of trees and flowers.

Great view of Florence from the top and no entrance fees. As I said about Rome, I mentioned the main points of this wonderful city, there is so much to see and do. Yet, sometimes slow down your tour, embrace the feel of the city you are visiting. Even sitting on a bench from time to time, just observing your surroundings, people passing by, nature, the scent of flowers or the aroma and flavors from a nearby bakery, little things like that, is time well spent!

Venezia
What an enchanting city Venice is! Truly one of a kind. I have traveled to many places and countries and there is nothing that can remotely compare to Venice. It is not just the canals; it is everything in and about Venice that makes it so unique! It only takes 4 hours by train from Rome, and Florence is pretty much halfway between the two cities. Get your camera or video ready before entering the lagoon by train, you certainly do not want to miss the spectacular view of the water on both sides as you approach Venice!

After arriving at the train stop at Santa Lucia station, you are just a few steps away from the vaporetti (waterbuses). I always enjoy the vaporetto rides, the scene that opens during the canal cruise is so fascinating. The beautiful building on both sides, some Gothic and some Renaissance style, the flowers on the balconies, the different shades of colors in the buildings, the great canal and the breeze make the trip not just a ride from point A to Point B, but an experience every time I am there. The ticket lasts 75 minutes so, depending on the route you choose, you may have time for a quick stop, take photos, and catch the next one along the way.

The easiest and fastest way to visit Venice is to simply take the vaporetto to Piazza San Marco (St Mark Square) and from there walk back to the other sites. There are several routes you can take depending on where you want to go. Most of them cross the Canal Grande, which is the largest and most important canal, and they also stop where the main touristic attractions are, such as the Ponte di Rialto, where I always get off to start my tour of this amazing and unique city.

The Rialto Bridge is one of the most beautiful monuments in Venice, the oldest of the 4 bridges that cross the Canal Grande, its architecture has the graceful artistic décor typical of the Renaissance period, but with its Venetian style.

Built at the end of 1500s, this stone bridge, with its many arches extending from side to side, providing structural strength to the bridge, gives the Rialto the added benefit of standing out in beauty, shape, and personality so to speak, giving it a very charming and romantic look. The bridge is also covered on top. Inside there are many jewelry and souvenir shops that make the crossing even more enjoyable, taking pictures of the bridge and the city from

different angles and, while you are at it, you might want to spend a bit of time looking at the beautiful merchandise on display to do some shopping.
I always start my tour of Venice from Ponte di Rialto (Rialto Bridge) not only because it is a beautiful location and a great starting point, but also because Venice is always full of tourists, so especially if I arrive early in the morning, the Ponte is not too crowded yet. From there I walk towards Piazza San Marco (St. Mark Square) and go to other historical places in the city deliberately choosing random streets and small alleys to reach my next destination, which is more interesting to me and less crowded. In other words, I start to wander, get lost and have fun! Venezia is not a big city and is very walkable, so no worries, if you get lost you can be "on your way" in no time.

Venice is a city famous all over the world for its canals, there are more than 150, and about 400 bridges, in addition to the most famous ones like Ponte di Rialto and Ponte dei Sospiri (Bridge of Sighs), there are many other smaller and beautiful bridges connecting one island to another. You will be so captivated and amazed by this fascinating city that you will not even notice that you are walking on so many small islands. (118 of them, to be precise).

Speaking of islands and bridges, you may be wondering why Ponte dei Sospiri has this unusual name. Although it is common to see couples kissing while taking pictures with the bridge in the background, there is no romance behind the meaning of this name as many people think. Instead, the sighs were those of the prisoners who knew that after crossing the bridge going into detention, they would most likely never see Venice (and be free) again.
Another bridge with an unusual name is Ponte dei Pugni (Bridge of Fists). This bridge is not large, nor does it have any artistic features, it is just a small, very ordinary looking bridge. The reason it is known is that in the 16th century, rival clans from different parts of Venice would occasionally meet in the middle of the bridge and engage in a fist fight.
The tradition had it that the winner would throw his opponent into the cold water of the canal, as the bridge had no railings. What remains of all that is a footstep mark on 2 sides of the bridge where the fighters had to put their foot.

Returning to our tour of this amazing and very romantic city, we continue towards the most iconic landmark of Venice, Piazza San Marco, Saint Mark Square. It is an impressive and historic square, with the Basilica of San Marco that is the emblem of Venice, known throughout the world. If you happen to find the square opening in front of you after being "lost" in some of the "calli" as they call their narrow alleys, the unexpected effect of the magnificent combination of landscape, sea, square, Basilica and Campanile, (Tower Bell) that you will have at first glance will be even more surprising and memorable. The monument that dominates St. Mark Square is St. Mark Basilica, is very imposing by size and the architecture is truly amazing. Completed in the year 1092, the façade of the church is a Gothic masterpiece, a rich composition of columns, arches, spires, crafts, and scenes of everyday life. It also shows an old man biting his hand. Legend has it that the man was the architect of the church removed from his position when he said he could build an even more beautiful one.

The structure of the church is enormous: five huge arches support five gigantic domes. Mosaics: the glow of golden mosaics, to achieve such a gorgeous effect the tiny squares of the mosaics tilt in different directions to better reflect the light from different angles. The winged lion: the winged lion is the symbol of Venice. In the Basilica is represented holding a Bible.

Campanile di San Marco (St. Mark Bell's Tower) This red brick structure was built during the 9th century but collapsed several times (also due to earthquakes). It was rebuilt and completed in 1912. It can be visited and walking up to the top is an amazing experience to enjoy an incredible view of Venice and its islands. Palazzo del Doge (Doge's Palace) is another impressive landmark in St. Mark Square. This Gothic style palace was built in 1340 and was the residence of the Doge of Venice, who centuries ago was the highest authority in Venice. Today Palazzo dei Dogi is an impressive museum, which showcases the history of the city and the lagoon as well as drawings of the interior rooms of the Palace.

What if, after admiring all the overwhelming beauty and charm of Venice, you feel the need for a break? You can certainly do this in one of the elegant cafes in Piazza San Marco. It might be a bit pricey to sit and enjoy an aperitif or a small brunch, but it comes with the view, yes sipping a drink comes with the view of one of the most amazing squares and sites in the world. Maybe even with a pianist in the background. This is perfection.

Now that I have mentioned a piano, the first thing that comes to my mind is il teatro La Fenice. This is an historic Opera House built in 1792 and has become very famous throughout Europe for the splendor of its building, which exudes class and elegance both in its exterior façade and in its interior decoration. It has a capacity of over 1000 seats. La Fenice Grand Theater (The Phoenix Grand Opera House) got its name because it was built on the site where another Opera House had previously been destroyed by fire; nevertheless, the owner decided to make the new Opera House even more grandiose than the previous one and named it Gran Teatro La Fenice. If you have the chance, an evening at the La Fenice would be an unforgettable experience during your stay in this truly unforgettable city.

Murano and Burano: Venice is known all over the world for its beautiful, delicate, and colorful Murano glass. If you want to know how glass is made and shaped, I recommend that you take a vaporetto to the Island of Murano and visit one of the small glass factories. You can attend (for a small fee) a glass making demonstration. You will learn how, in just few minutes, skilled artisans transform a piece of glass into an artistic craft. If you like laces, Burano is the island to go to. In addition, Burano has a very colorful neighborhood, with brightly colored houses, a great place for photos, and easy to walk around. If you like both islands, well, you know what to do!

If you go to Venice in the summer and want to spend a day at the beach you can, just take a vaporetto to the Lido di Venezia. There you can sunbathe both in the free beaches and in the equipped ones that offer all the comforts such as sun lounger, umbrella and so on. At the Lido you can also escape the crowded tourist areas and enjoy a quieter day. Unless you go in September, then it will not be so quiet. Not at all.

Every year, at the beginning of September and for about 10 days, the Lido hosts La Biennale di Venezia, Venice International Film Festival, one of the oldest, most glamorous, and star-studded film events in the world. Hundreds of journalists, TV crews from all over the world, non-stop interviews, film promotions, exclusives galas and much more take place at the Lido. And of course, crowds of fans hoping to see their favorite actors.

Ah, so much glamour! At the Venice Film Festival, celebrities and glamour go hand in hand with a place that is a reference in Venice in its category: Hotel Danieli. This historic and prestigious 5 stars hotel, sets the bar very high even when compared to other luxury hotels around the world. Palazzo Danieli was built at the end of the 14th century.

The Gothic exterior façade, the imposing opulence of the atrium and staircase, the magnificent halls with the typical Venetian style chandeliers, sumptuous, frescoed ceilings, a breathtaking view from the terrace of the lagoon and the islands and, of course, Piazza San Marco.

It has a private entrance into the water by boat, you understand why I say it sets the standards for all other 5-star hotels very high. Add to everything I have just described, the "little detail" that you could be sleeping in a Palace that is over 500 years old. Where else in the world can you compare yourself to or approach to live an experience like that of being a guest at the Hotel Danieli? Historical figures, celebrities from the past and recent years have slept in this hotel, including many of those who attended the Venice International Film Festival. In case you are wondering, I have not yet been a guest at the Danieli.

From my experience, the best part of being in Venice is, being in Venice! This city is so unique that it gives you the opportunity to do things you could not do anywhere else, simply because there is no other place that is built on 118 tiny islands, and the only way to get around is on foot or by boat. You will never see a car there (ambulances are also boats).
Just your feet, the vaporetto or a romantic gondola, which yes, it can be a little pricey but romantic, and the gondolier can take you through small canals and maybe tell you stories or anecdotes about the area. So, take advantage of it, explore it as much as possible, walk the tiny alleys, when you make a turn, you may find your own "discovery".

I remember when I was in Venice years ago, wandering around these little streets and looking for a place to dine outside of the crowded and touristy area. Eventually I saw a quaint little restaurant on the corner of a little side street. We walked in and the waiter led the way to our table.
When we sat down, he asked us if we wanted to open the blinds to get more sunlight, we said yes and when he opened them, what a scene! A small balcony full of colorful flowers overlooking a canal, about a meter (3 feet) from us and a small bridge in the background. What a "discovery". A perfect place we knew nothing about, I still have the picture of that moment, all smiles.

Look at the buildings where people live, try to imagine what it is like to live a day-to-day life in Venice, with its uniqueness and its challenges. Then you will feel as you have not only visited Venezia, but also experienced it!

CITIES AND TOWNS TOTALLY WORTH VISITING

In addition to the three main cities to visit if you only have few days of vacation, there are many beautiful towns that, if you have the time, are worth a visit. Some of them are big cities like Milan and Naples which are mostly famous for other reasons rather than their historical background.
Milan is world famous for its fashion designers, and therefore this city is called the "fashion capital". It is also the most important financial and commercial district in Italy.

Naples is most famous for its delicious Neapolitan pizza. Pizza was invented in Naples and even today, pizza is an institution in the daily life of this city. It is also famous for the world known song "O sole mio" written in 1898, and of course, for being the starting point for the enchanting island of Capri and the Amalfi coast. However, these two cities are much more than that, and both have interesting historical points, so let's take a closer look at these two important cities.

Milano

This rich and sophisticated city has at least three great historical sites that are a must see even if you are in Milan for a short time. The most famous and impressive is the Duomo di Milano in piazza del Duomo. This Gothic cathedral, whose construction began in 1386, when the Gothic style was at its peak, represents the most important landmark of this thriving city.
This cathedral is said to have more statues than any other building in the world, around 3400 statues and 700 figures have been inserted to decorate it, an impressive number indeed, as impressive are the architectural details on its walls. Due to the massive and intricate details in it, this project took centuries to complete. The Duomo is by far the most iconic monument for which Milan is best known for.

Another imposing monument located less than a mile from the Duomo, is the Castello Sforzesco. This fortress, built in the 15th century, was known as Castello di Porta Giova and renamed in honor of the Duke of Milan Francesco Sforza who rebuilt and enlarged it. The Castello Sforzesco (Sforza Castle) is now home to different types of museums, by style and theme: from the Museum of Decorative Arts to the Egyptian Museum to name a couple. It also houses Michelangelo's last masterpiece, La Pieta'. With so much to see and do all in one place, you can easily spend the entire day at the castle, for a complete cultural experience. The Castle features a beautiful internal courtyard, and is connected to the largest park in Milan, Parco Sempione, with paths, ponds and the beautiful Porta Sempione, with the Arco della Pace, reminiscent of the Arc de Triomphe in Paris. The monument Arco della Pace, (Arch of Peace), whose history begins with the celebration of the wedding between Eugenio di Beauharnais, adopted son of Napoleon and viceroy of Italy, with Augusta of Bavaria, in 1806. The arch it was a symbol of welcome for newlyweds in the city.

Other important historical events happened soon after, and when the Arch was completed in 1815 it was dedicated to peace among the European nations in 1815 at the Congress of Vienna. The monument shows above a group of bronze statues, with four victories on horseback. The front shows the personifications of the Adda, Po, Tagliamento and Ticino rivers.

Milano is the capital of the fashion industry, so spending some time in Milan for luxury shopping is almost a must. What better place to do it than Galleria Vittorio Emanuele II? No matter what the weather is like, cold or hot, rain or shine, this historic Galleria is an indoor shopping mall and the oldest in Italy. Approximately 150 years old, it looks just as elegant and glamourous as it did when it first opened. Named after the King Vittorio Emanuele II, the structure is made up of glass, arches, glass domes and a double-arched, glass vaulted passage that connects two of Milan's main squares: Piazza del Duomo and Piazza della Scala. The high walls are also adorned with paintings.

Inside the Galleria there are not only branded shops, but also café', restaurants, bookstores and even a hotel. Very entertaining to look out of the hotel room down to the ground floor and see all the happening downstairs: people walking, some enjoying an aperitivo and others going in and out the stores. It is in heart of Milano's city center, in front of the Duomo.

The Galleria is not the only place for high-end shopping: via Monte Napoleone, just few minutes' walk from it, is the street where you can find your favorite Italian (and not only Italian) designer store.

The words upscale, glamour and Milan, marry perfectly with something else that in Milan is synonymous with glamour and refined: the celebrated Teatro alla Scala, or simply La Scala.

This sumptuous Opera House is the most prestigious Italian Opera House known internationally. It was built by Empress Maria Theresa of Austria (Austria ruled Milan at the time) and was inaugurated in 1778 (14 years before la Fenice in Venice). It has a capacity of 2000 seats. Among the major composers who have performed at La Scala in the last 200 years, there are Arturo Toscanini, Giuseppe Verdi, Giacomo Puccini and Niccolo' Paganini. Even in modern times, the best Opera singers and ballet dancers from all over the world have performed at La Scala.

For a much more casual night, the Milanesi love to go to the Navigli. The Navigli of Milan are a system of navigable canals crossing the city. These canals are both natural and artificial, connecting Milan to Lake Maggiore, Lake Como, the River Po, becoming an outlet on the Adriatic Sea. Furthermore, to Ticino River in Switzerland, which connects its waters with northern Europe.
The system started long, long ago, during the Middle Ages in the 12th century, to protect Milan in case of invasion and to have a supply of water available for the city. The first canal was inaugurated in 1179.
Centuries later even Leonardo Da Vinci took part at this enormous project with his genius idea of a system of locks, he completed a complex hydraulic work, and was able to connect Milan with Lake Como.
As I said, the Milanese love the Navigli, during the day busy people go there to grab a bite to eat during their lunch break and in the evening to stroll, do some shopping, for an aperitif or dinner in bars and restaurants located for miles along the Navigli and maybe end the evening in one of the clubs.

For a cultural day in Milan, La Pinacoteca di Brera, (the Brera Art Gallery) is an excellent choice. Housed in a beautiful and elegant former convent building, with an internal courtyard, a portico along the perimeter with columns and arches typical of a monastery before becoming a museum. Since 1776 it has been the most important and famous public art gallery in Milan.
The collections are very rich with some of the most famous works in the world: one of the masterpieces of the Pinacoteca di Brera is the painting of the Kiss by Hayez. What intense romanticism in the painting! The collections have works by Braque, Modigliani, Picasso and many others.

Napoli

Not many cities in the world are in such a wonderful geographical position as Naples. Picture this image in your mind: it is located on a beautiful bay, facing the Tyrrhenian Sea, embraced by the Gulf of Naples and Mount Vesuvio behind, which is not just an "ordinary" mountain, but a volcano.
Quite out of the ordinary indeed. If that is not enough, from Naples you can see the shape of the island of Procida, as well as both edges of the Bay of Naples, and the enchanting, world-famous, picturesque island of Capri!

The first time I visited Naples, the monument I liked the most was Castel dell'Ovo (Castle of the Egg). Positioned in a very scenic location, directly on the sea and connected to the mainland by a small bridge, the imposing structure of the castle itself, the bay, the charming restaurants nearby practically on the water, everything was just so beautiful, it became one my favorite places. In front of the walls is the small harbor Borgo Marinari, home to various nautical clubs. Up to this day (I have been to Naples many other times since then, will say more about it) is the 1st landmark I look for when I arrive. What a curious name, Castle of the Egg, I thought to myself.

Let me tell you the interesting and fascinating story of this castle, surrounded by a thousand-year history and a legend. Long before the foundation of Castel dell'Ovo, a Roman Patrician named Licinio Lucullo saw an islet called Magaride almost attached to the mainland by a multitude of small rocks.
Realizing the enormous potential of the place, he had a magnificent, grandiose villa built, or as the Ancient Romans call it in Latin, Castellum Lucullanum (Lucullan Castle). In his sumptuous castle, Lucullus exploiting his great wealth, gave life to historical and philosophical studies, various entertainments, endless banquets, dances, and other excesses that created the adjective "lucullan" to indicate this showy and lavish way of life.
Centuries later, from the fifth to the tenth century, the castle became a hermitage for Basilian monks. From showy display of one means of life to a hermitage for monks…. Quite a drastic change, isn't it?

Over the centuries however, the castle suffered several attacks, changing its shape to a certain extent, and was repeatedly partially rebuilt and even renamed by the last conqueror. In 1128 it was given the shape we can still admire today. But why was it called Castel dell'Ovo, Castel of the Egg, you may wonder. This is where the legend comes into play.
It is said in an ancient legend that its name derives from having the Latin poet Virgilio hidden in the Castle a sort of "special" egg that was supposed to keep the fortress safe. According to the legend, he placed the egg in a vase inside an iron cage and hid it in the basement of the Castle where the prison was located. If the egg had broken, it would have caused the collapse of the castle, and it would also have meant disasters for Naples.
Virgil despite being from northern Italy, among other cities also lived in Naples for years, which already at that time had a large population and problems with the surrounding terrain, including some swamps infested with disease-carrying insects. It so happened that Virgilio was a good connoisseur of the subject having learned from his father, a landowner and a farmer, he directed

many reclamations works. Using his influence and skills, he managed to solve problems that for centuries burdened the live of Neapolitans, who, not knowing that it was thanks to his agricultural competence that he solved them, began to consider Virgilio, now a resident of Naples, as a special person also able to protect the city through an egg inside a hidden iron cage.

The rumors about Virgil's egg in the castle emerged however, in the late Middle Ages and Castel dell'Ovo was a name already mentioned in documents of the 13th century on which it was written that in the prior century King Roger the Norman rebuilt the castle from pre-existing ruins giving it an oval shape. Moreover, from documents found by Neapolitan scholars, it emerged that it was precisely the oval shape of the castle that gave it the name of Castel dell'Ovo. By the way, despite numerous searches carried out throughout the castle centuries ago, the iron cage containing the egg was never found, obviously confirming that this was a centuries-old hearsay legend.

Castel dell'Ovo has a free admission to visit it. From the top floor you can enjoy an incredible view of Naples and the gulf, an ideal place for amazing pictures. As for Licinio Lucullo grand villa, or Castellum Lucullanum, some ruins can be seen in the basement of Castel dell'Ovo and more recently, large ruins have been discovered and brought to light in piazza Municipio, about 20 minutes on foot from the original castle. If you would like to see the new ruins (a bit odd writing these two words next to each other, new ruins), if you are thinking that 20 minutes of walking might be too long or boring, the reality is far from it! There is such a wealth of history and monuments in this 20-minute walk between Castle of the Egg and piazza Municipio that if you were to tour them it could easily take the whole day to get there. Let's go!

After exiting Castel dell'Ovo keep to the right and continue the beautiful walkway of via Partenope (which will turn into via Nazario Sauro). The view of the sea, the breeze, looking at the restaurants across the street will make this short walk very pleasant along the way. Turn left on via Cesario Console and 1 minute later you will arrive at the largest and most grandiose square in Napoli: Piazza del Plebiscito. Inaugurated in 1846, this enormous piazza, with its colonnade on both sides, houses two of the main monuments of the city: Basilica San Francesco da Paola (built in 1816) with its dome and columns resembling the Pantheon in Rome, and on the opposite side, Palazzo Reale, (the Royal Palace). Being very spacious, it makes it the perfect location for gathering and concerts in the city.

The Royal Palace of Naples. When I visited the Royal Palace just a few years ago, it was one of those wow moments. I was strolling in Piazza Plebiscito with my mother and daughter, we were looking at exterior façade of this large

structure when my mother said, "why don't we go inside and tour it?". I didn't know much about the Palace apart that it was residence of the King of Naples. From the outside the building is very prominent, and its appearance has a sobriety about it, something in between elegant and somewhat austere at the same time, but when walked in...we were blown away.
The grand marble staircase, statues carved into the pink marble walls, arches and balconies everywhere, the designs on the pavements and the décor in the ceiling, what a moment. We did not expect anything like that.

That was just the entrance. Built in 1600, this sumptuous residence is an outstanding expression of the Renaissance style in its interiors, and later some Baroque décor were also added. It was first the residence of the Spanish Viceroys, then the Borbonica dynasty from 1743 and finally as a Neapolitan residence for the kings of the Savoia dynasty.
In 1919 the King of Vittorio Emanuele III of Savoia ceded the Palace to the State Property and part of it is largely used as a National Library (which, with over two million texts, is the most important library in Southern Italy and among the first in the world). The oldest wing became the Royal Palace Museum. Inside the Palace it is possible to visit the Royal Apartment which has numerous rooms (including the Court Theatre and the Throne Room). Exquisite chandeliers, decors, paintings, statues, vaulted ceilings, well describe the magnificence of the residence of the King and Queen.

What struck me even more, however, were the spectacular views from all sides: imagine opening the balcony on one side of the Palace that overlooks the imposing Piazza Plebiscito, on the other side the balcony opens onto an enchanting hanging garden full of flowers and trees of different styles, benches and beautiful paths, on the third side a terrace to sit outside and enjoy the incredible view of the sea and the bay of Naples, which at night is even more delightful with the lights of the city and, last but not least, mount Vesuvio can be seen from afar on the fourth side of the Palace. Simply amazing. I cannot imagine a more perfect location for a Royal Palace.

There is more: The Royal Summer Residence, La Reggia di Caserta. (The Royal Palace of Caserta). I will go into more detail later in the book. Now, after the royal experience of visiting and admiring the magnificence of a Royal House, we decided to continue this regal moment by visiting the annexed Teatro Reale di San Carlo, The Royal Opera House of St. Charles.
Yes, the Kings not only had their own private Court Theater but attached to the Royal Palace is also a Royal Opera House (of course, the royals had their

own private entrance and royal box seating with golden curtains, in the most prominent area of the Opera House, with the best view of the stage and hall). The Royal Opera House of San Carlo was commissioned by the King Carlo di Borbone and inaugurated in 1737, decades before the other two Opera Houses, I mentioned earlier, La Scala in Milan, (1778) and La Fenice in Venice (1792). It is the oldest and continuously active Opera House in the world.

It originally had over 3000 seats, but in modern times it has been reduced to about half (due to new security coding for fire alarms, electrical system etc). The interior and decoration of the hall is sumptuous: frescoes on the ceiling, royal coats of arms, the architecture of the hall itself exude finesse and majesty in every detail. In 1800 composers of the caliber of Rossini and Verdi wrote some of their masterpiece purposely for the San Carlo Orchestra. The Opera House is certainly one of the must-see attractions in Napoli. Even better, not just visit it, experience an evening at the Opera! As for the 3 of us who wanted to visit it, it was closed that day. Bummer....

Once outside the Opera House if you look across the street, you can see the Galleria Umberto I, a beautiful and classy shopping arcade and eatery. It was built in 1887 and has a design and structure similar to those of Milan and Rome. A few steps from the Opera House on the same busy street, there it is, with its imposing presence, Castel Nuovo, also knowns as il Maschio Angioino. Built in 1279, this imponent Medieval structure, is another of the historical landmarks of Naples.
This ponderous Castle with an austere appearance, embellished with five cylindrical towers, seems to dominate the entire city. It was built as a residence and a defensive fortress. Over time, this massive castle has undergone some changes on the façade, and now has beautiful marble arch with Latin inscriptions, statues and figures at the entrance, which give it light and a less austere appearance. The Maschio Angioino like most castles, has a large museum with different exhibitions that change from time to time. By the way.... this Castle is in Piazza Municipio! Next to the Castle is the excavation for the "new" ruins of Licinio Lucullo. Quite an interesting itinerary this 20-minute walk from Castel dell'Ovo, isn't it?

Another castle in Naples even more imposing and austere than the Maschio Angioino, is located at about 35 minutes on foot from Piazza Municipio. This time no walking itinerary, especially because the road to reach this castle is quite uphill. Better to use a cab or public transport. When I went, I took the funicular, a 5-minute ride on a cable car, up to the Vomero neighborhood, from the last stop I walked for about 10 minutes, and this gigantic and massive fortress, Castel Sant' Elmo (St. Elmo Castle) was right in front of me.

St. Elmo, a mighty military fortress built in the 1300s during Medieval times, is in a very strategic position: on the highest hill of Naples, at about 250 meter or 820 feet, it offers an extraordinary panoramic view of the Gulf of Naples and Mount Vesuvius. It dominates the entire city from every angle, far and wide. The view is so wide that it allows you to recognize the different districts of Naples... if you know them!

The long, straight and narrow street, famous because it is said to divide the city into two parts, called Spaccanapoli (Naples' splitter) is easily recognizable from that high point (ok, it took me few seconds to find it...at first glance). On the way back from the castle, the descent is effortless, and can be done simply by strolling down the characteristic alleys of Vomero all the way to sea level.

Another suggestive area is Posillipo. Spread over a hillside coastline, this upscale residential area is known for its beautiful private villas, some of which built in the 18th and 19th centuries, an archeological park with Roman ruins and spectacular views of the bay from a different angle with view on the island of Nisida. Posillipo is also known for its seafood restaurants and beautiful beaches along the coast. One that I particularly like is the beach and small bay of "Bagno Sirena". Pastel colored buildings by the sea on one side, and palazzo Donn'Anna, a historic residence literally on the water's edge on the other side, with the beautiful view of the Gulf of Naples in the distance, make this lovely place the perfect spot for a beach day without even leaving the city.

Beautiful beaches right in the heart of the city, the archeological park at the top, but how about a "regular" park for jogging, bike riding, picnicking, is there even that? Obviously! And it is not just a "regular" park: located at the top of Capodimonte hill, Capodimonte Park not only is an oasis of peace and tranquility in the midst of a big city, but it is so well laid out it's just a pleasure to take the time to visit.

While you're enjoying the view of Naples and its bay, you may also want to visit the historic building that was one of the residences of King Borbone, the man who built the Royal Palace and the Reggia di Caserta also built the Royal Forest of Capodimonte, now turned into a public park and his residence in a museum that displays exhibits, paintings, frescos, porcelains and, of course, the sumptuous interior rooms where the Royals lived. Capodimonte indeed is not just a "regular" park.

Aside from touring the city and learning about the monuments and historical landmarks, one thing I always try to do when I travel is to get a feel for the city

I am visiting, perceiving the culture inherent in it. The easiest way to do this, is to simply walk along some pedestrian streets in different areas if time permits, not so much to look at the storefronts, but at the area, the buildings and people passing by, to get a feel for that place. In Naples my favorite street is Via Chiaia. It runs from Piazza Trieste and Trento (next to Piazza Plebiscito) to Piazza dei Martiri. It is less crowded than the parallel and wider via Toledo. Halfway through via Chiaia, a bridge (not passable from there) built in 1636, Ponte di Chiaia with a beautiful white arch, connects two areas above.

On occasions, I stopped in front of the arch to listen to the talented street artists in the area who played famous pop song with the violin, giving them such a different and beautiful "flavor". The violin makes each song so evocative and captivating. Day after day from 6:00 pm you can be almost certain that the skilled player is there to entertain the passersby with the gentle sound of the violin and a hat on the ground for appreciative listeners.

Before arriving at piazza dei Martiri, the street becomes a little wider with trees on both sides, giving an even nicer touch of green color to the surrounding area, providing some shade as you sit on the benches to relax and enjoy the moment. The nice shops and small restaurants nearby complement the pretty sight. I never tire of walking down Via Chiaia, and although the street is always busy full of locals walking and chatting, there is still a pleasant sense of tranquility.

Naples is a city full of contrast, breathtaking landscapes that the world envies us and sites that need a lot of renovations. Many years ago, when I went to Naples, I would stop at a few places or go to the islands.

My daughter and her husband moved to Napoli a few years ago. They both love to explore and discover every new place on their path. They saw great potential in a large city like Naples. She can always find something different, interesting or particular about a place, and her husband has a great talent for taking photos that capture the beauty and character of it. Visiting them and showing me their "discoveries" gave me the opportunity to learn more about this city. I look forward to going back when I am in Italy. Napoli is a fascinating city, also because of its contrasts.

Speaking of fascinating, a trip to this area is not complete without going to its amazing islands (more about on the Seaside Places chapter) and to Pompeii, the village and its inhabitants buried under the ashes of the eruption of Mount Vesuvio in 79 A.D.

Pompei and nearby Ercolano are two very interesting and fascinating places to visit, you will see that everything is still well preserved just as it was at the time when the eruption occurred. Info on **www.pompeiisites.org**

In this chapter of the book, I delved first into Milan and Naples because they are the two largest cities in Italy besides Rome. Going forward, the cities and towns will be listed in geographical order, from North to South.

Torino

Turin is a city often overlooked by tourists, perhaps because of its proximity (1 hour by train) to the more famous Milan, Turin is indeed a beautiful and elegant city with a lot to offer in terms of tourism, art, culture, and of course, its regional cuisine. There are many historical testimonies that have occurred over the centuries; the massive Porta Palatina, built in the 1st century AD testifies to the belonging of Turin to the Roman Empire. For centuries it was the ancient capital of the king of Savoy, contributing to shape it the way it looks today. It is decorated with Renaissance and Baroque architecture that can been seen in its monuments, buildings and piazzas such as the beautiful piazza San Carlo. It boasts more than 40 museums, it is known for its jewels and, of course, for being an industrial capital, Fiat Auto is based in Turin.

Arriving in Turin, one the first things that stands out from different parts of the city is the imposing chain of the Alps in the background with its snow- capped peaks visible for much of the year.

The most famous monument and symbol of Turin is undoubtedly La Mole Antonelliana, Built in 1863, this unique, impressive building of monumental proportion stands 167 meters high (550 feet), is the tallest brick building in Turin, from its top you can enjoy a stunning view of the city and the mountains. It was a monument dedicated to the king of Savoy. Since 2000, La Mole has housed the National Museum of Cinema and it hosts events and exhibits throughout the year. Piazza Castello (Castle's Square) is another landmark of Turin. This large, beautiful and regal square is also home to the Palazzo Reale. The Royal Palace, built in 1646, was the main place of residence of the King. The splendor of its façade, the lavish decorations of the rooms, ceilings and furniture, represented the majesty of the Savoy's dynasty. Palazzo Reale is not the only building in Piazza Castello. Palazzo Madama (Lady's Palace) in Baroque style, once a fortress, was the residence of two Royal Madams. The Palace with its imposing staircase, is now a museum. Castle and Park of Valentino is an example of splendor in the heart of the city center and is listed as UNESCO World Heritage Site. The beautiful park surrounding the castle, makes visiting the area even more enjoyable. Inside the park there is a small, pretty village built in 1884 in Medieval style for an exhibition, people liked the village so much that it was decided to keep it, a nice place to take pictures. Among the over 40 museums in Turin there is one that never changes its theme: the Egyptian Museum. This museum is solely dedicated to showcasing the art, culture and manufacts of the ancient Egypt, it has over 30000 pieces, including statues of pharaohs. Turin's historic district is also very pleasant for a stroll through its many arcades, elegant stores and pastry shops, it is always a good time to sip the bicerin, a hot drink made of coffee, chocolate and milk cream, sample Turin's signature chocolate the gianduiotto, a slice of the bonet cake, or the very sweet marron glace' (glazed chestnut). Turin's passion for food is not only sweet delicacies: the central market in Porta Palazzo area has become more sophisticated with the new indoor hub, three floors of gourmet food for a total gastronomic experience. For refined tastes, the exclusive historic ristorante Del Cambio, open since 1757. Dining in their grand halls with sumptuous chandeliers is an experience in itself. Speaking of sumptuous, 10 km from Turin is the Reggia di Venaria, a majestic royal palace with gardens, built in 1675 as one of the residences of the Royal House of Savoy. A must see.

Verona

I really like Verona and for many reasons. This city lies in a very convenient position, close to Venice and Padua on the east side, beautiful lake Garda with its many charming towns on the west side, and the Dolomites on the North side. Perfect location for many day trips to visit other cities or to be in the countryside. The city itself is charming and very walkable in the old historic district, as all the tourist attractions are close to each other.
Verona's most famous landmark is the Arena, the ancient amphitheater built by the Romans. Opera singer Luciano Pavarotti has performed many times at the Arena, Italy's largest Opera House. This mini-Colosseum, built in 30 AD, is a striking location for operas or concerts, but it also offer superb acoustics.
The main square of the city is the lively piazza Bra, with restaurants all around and the Arena dominating the square. The Portoni della Bra, a beautiful piece of 14th century architecture with two arches, is the southern entrance to the old city in piazza Bra. The area is even prettier at night when all the lights give a more intimate and warmer atmosphere to the square and its landmarks.
Other landmarks are the Ponte Scaligero, completed in 1356, also called Ponte Castelvecchio due to its proximity to Castello Castelvecchio (Oldcastle Castle). The castle, a beautiful example of Mediaeval architecture, was built in the 14th century. Like many other castles in Italy, it has become a museum.
Inside the ancient walls there are two famous squares: one is piazza dei Signori (Lord's square), with its beautiful and important medieval buildings. These include the 12th century Palazzo della Ragione (Palace of Reason), the one crossed by 2 horizontal lines and with a tall tower, the Lamberti tower. For a

small fee you can enjoy an incredible view from the top of Verona, its limpid river Adige, and the mighty chain of the Dolomites in the distance. The other square is piazza delle Erbe (Herbs Square), built in 1368 received this name because, centuries ago the square housed a market selling herbs and spices. This historical square is smaller than the others but equally charming with its classy buildings and arcades all around.

One last thing about Verona: are you a romantic type? Yes, no, or not very much? Verona is the location of one of the most famous love stories in the world, Shakespeare's play Romeo and Juliet, so if you answered no or not very much, this is your chance to be romantic for a few minutes.

You could take your spouse or future spouse to the famous Juliet's balcony where one of the most romantic scenes in the play takes place, and recite what Romeo said to her beloved Juliet: "But wait, what's that light in the window over there? It is the east, and Juliet is the sun. Rise up, beautiful sun, and kill the jealous moon. The moon is already sick and pale with grief because you, Juliet, her maid, are more beautiful than she".

Awww so much romance and drama in just a few words, what a romantic moment to "improvise"! So, what do you say, will this poetic date going to happen? All I will say is:

Visiting Juliet's house costs a small fee,
admiring Juliet's balcony is free,
but this is not a cheap date indeed,
reciting Romeo's words to your AMORE is a priceless…deed!

Padova

"Venezia la bella e Padova sua sorella", Venice the beautiful and Padua its sister, so goes an old popular proverb, which gives an idea of the charm and the historical heritage that Padua has to offer to visitors who come to this ancient city. Between two large cities, about 30 miles from Venice and 60 from Verona, all three with their uniqueness, blend and complete each other at the same time. These cities are a cradle of historical heritage of solid importance, where past and present form a pleasant unison to be seen and lived in everyday life, the ancient with the modern, the medieval and Renaissance buildings close to the universities with an eye for art, culture, and science.

The same is true for gastronomy. The most famous dish in Padova is hundreds of years old, the substantial comfort food gallina padovana, the Paduan hen. Padova is also the birthplace of the famous aperitivo Spritz, a delicious cocktail drink that in just a few years has become so popular that it has spread throughout Italy and beyond its borders.

Padova has quite a few places that are so historically and architecturally striking that they have become landmarks of Padova. Sant'Antonio da Padova Basilica, an imposing structure that laid its first stone in medieval times. What makes the Basilica particularly interesting from an artistic point of view is the coexistence of the most diverse styles that have followed one another in different eras. The Romanesque façade, the seven Gothic chapels, the Byzantine domes, and the Moorish bell tower blend beautifully together, making the Basilica one of the most famous and visited monuments in Padua.

The Prato della Valle square is another place very dear to the locals and one of the symbols of Padova. For many reasons. Firstly, its size, this square is extraordinarily large, about 90000 square meters, second only to the Red Square in Moscow by extension. It is so big that there was enough space to build an island in the middle!

Yes, an islet, Isola Memmia, in honor of the mayor who commissioned the massive project, with a canal (of a nearby river whose waters are connected by an underground tunnel) all around connected to the "mainland" through 4 pedestrian bridges. The canal is decorated with 78 statues all-around of famous local characters from the past.

The area itself was used by the Ancient Romans as an open-air theater and as a market in medieval time the square had its first foundation in 1638 although over the centuries it underwent numerous restorations and embellishments.

Piazza delle Erbe and the adjacent Piazza della Frutta (Square of the Herbs and Square of the Fruits) are two beautifully adorned squares in the historic district of Padova. As the names explain, they have been used as market squares for many centuries up to this day.

These squares are not only markets though, but they are also home to important and historical palaces such as the Palazzo della Ragione (Palace of the Reason), a medieval building of great and majestic beauty, used as the Palace of Justice (therefore the term Reason is very appropriate). The Palace, built in 1218, is impressive in size and architecture with arches on both floors. An abundance of frescos, paintings, artifacts and statues fill the interiors of this museum. From the 2nd floor you can enjoy a beautiful view of the bustling square. On the ground floor there are different types of shops run by local artisans. Both squares, Piazza delle Erbe and Piazza della Frutta are always very lively no matter what time of day or evening you arrive. During the day there are usually markets with stalls selling produce and other edibles, while in the afternoon until dusk you can see people strolling or sitting for an aperitivo at the bars in the piazza and, in the evening, it turns into an outdoor dining area with its many restaurants. Whenever you get there, it will always be a pleasant sight to see and enjoy.

Palazzo Bo is another important building just a few minutes' walk from Piazza delle Erbe. This Palace, which is a university of historical significance, laid its foundation in 1222, has been in operation ever since, and celebrates its 800th anniversary in 2022. Quite a milestone indeed. It was at this university that the world's first woman graduated in 1678. The Palace and its courtyard can be visited every day of the week.

Bassano del Grappa and Marostica

These two quaint little towns in the Veneto region, near the city of Vicenza, are off the beaten path of the typical tourist destination. However, both towns are beautiful to look at, have historical landmarks, enjoyable to visit, and both are famous for two very different reasons:

Bassano del Grappa: this old town is known for its beautiful wooden covered bridge Ponte Vecchio (Old Bridge). Built in 1209, it looks good for its age. I remember walking back and forth on this very solid bridge and hearing the impetuous sound of waters (at least on that day) of the river below, it was fun. Bassano del Grappa it is also famous for its...yes grappa, a very strong brandy that the locals drink (in small quantities and as quickly as a shot) especially during their long, cold winter.

Marostica: before telling you a little about this town, I have a question for you: do you play chess? If so, you will love Marostica! If not, I am sure you will still enjoy the story you are about to read. So, read on!

Marostica, a small quaint, old-fashioned village not far from Bassano, is world famous for its living chess game. Yes, a living chess game! Every even year in September (this started after World War I), members of the local chess club started playing chess in the main square using people as the game pieces, all dressed up in such a way as to recognize what chess piece they represent.

An unusual and interesting thing to watch even for non-chess lovers like me, who do not play chess. (I did enjoy taking pictures of the chess floor though) What I really love about this living chess game is the story of how it started. It was the year 1454. Two noblemen, Rinaldo d'Angarano and Vieri da Vallonara, are both in love with Lionora, the beautiful daughter of Taddeo Parisio, Lord of the Manor. As it is the custom back then, the two men decide to fight a duel for the right to seek Lionora's hand.

Her father, the Lord of the Manor, who has spies everywhere, finds out about the duel and forbids it. "No pain and blood to have my daughter's hand" he says! Instead, he decided the matter to be determined on a different way, by a chess match, to be held on September 12th of that year. The winner will marry Lionora, and the loser will marry Oldrada, Lionora's younger sister. Both are known to be excellent chess players and they eagerly accept the Lord's proposal. Lionora, who is secretly in love with one of the men, is distraught, she cannot help thinking and fearing she could see her sister married to the man she loves!

The match will take place at the Castle's courtyard on a specially set up chessboard. After the game, there will be a feast with fireworks and dancing to celebrate the wedding to be of the two daughters.

Lionora anxiously keep peeking from a window overlooking the courtyard. She had told her servant if the man she loves wins the match she would put a candle by the window as a signal to the people to share her joy.

The game is over. Vieri da Vallonara is the winner. Lionora is going to marry Vieri. The celebration starts and two weddings are about to take place. By the way, a candle burns by the window where Lionora had watched the game.

What a romantic love story! And Lionora's father what a smart and wise person. He changed the Medieval rule of duels full of blood and death with a much intriguing one, a duel on a chess game!

I hope you enjoyed this story, maybe now you have one more reason to visit Marostica. Now, let us continue to visit other places of this beautiful country!

Trieste

Trieste is a port city located at the eastern end of Italy, on the border with Slovenia. This beautiful city of Friuli e Venezia Giulia region is mostly known for its cold wind, the bora, which, over time (in the winter months) batters the city at hurricane force winds up to 100 miles per hour.

The Triestini inhabitants are used to this gale force wind. At times, growing up in Italy, I remember seeing on the news, videos of this incredible strong wind and of people literally being caught by it, clinging to the light pole (a scene seen many times on tv) so as not to be swept away.

There is much more to Trieste to being only known for its bora wind or for being a border city. In fact, I have been always so curious about Trieste that few years ago I went there to visit it.

Flying there from Rome was a good choice, the plane flew over Venice and its lagoon and, sitting by the window, gave me the opportunity to take some nice

pictures of the lagoon and its hundreds of islands. Even arriving at the very small and organized airport, it was a breeze (talking about... winds) to take a bus from there to Trieste.
What a pleasant surprise Trieste was. Starting with one of its most famous landmarks, the main square Piazza Unita' d'Italia (Unity of Italy Square). I had seen it in photos and videos before I went there and knew it was a big square, but I didn't expect to be so beautiful, impressive, and so enormous! So much so that is the largest seaside square in Europe. When the square was built centuries ago, it was less than half the size it is today.

For a long time, Trieste and the surrounding area was part of the Austro-Hungarian rule, while more recently, after World War II, the area that is now part of Slovenia belonged to Italy. The square overlooks the sea and is surrounded by historical buildings and palaces. Going clockwise from the seaside there are the following: Palace of the Austrian Lieutenancy built in 1905, now the Prefecture headquarter. Palazzo Stratti built in 1839. Palazzo Modello built in 1871. The Municipio (City Hall) built in 1875.
A very interesting detail about this Palace is its architecture, structured and built in such a way that it combines other pre-existing buildings on either side into one, more grandiose building. I would have never guessed it; it takes great skills and ingenuity to accomplish such a large task. On the tower, two bronze automatons make their chimes heard at the stroke of the hour.
The palace next to the City Hall is Palazzo Pitteri. Built in 1780 is the oldest palace in Piazza Unita'. The last two buildings are Grand Hotel Duchi di Aosta built in 1873, and the headquarter of Friuli Venezia Region, built in 1884. The overall view from the sea of this prestigious square and its palaces is a spectacular one, even more so at night. A short walk from the square is an area called Borgo Teresiano. This district dates to the reign of Empress Maria Teresa (hence the name). The grand canal that runs through it, the nearby streets, some historic buildings, shops, restaurants, make it the perfect place to stroll where the locals meet for a nice lunch.

On a nice walk uphill from the square is the Castle of San Giusto and its Cathedral. Imposing in their structure typical of the Medieval era, built in 1328. Both buildings have an austere appearance and presence. The Cathedral has a beautiful large rose window that softens the façade. A short walk to the nearby large terrace allows you to enjoy a beautiful view of the city below.
After lunch, while wandering around, I noticed a cable car (by the way, Trieste is very hilly, wear comfy shoes) that had Opicina as its destination. I thought it was a cute name, so being curious by nature, I asked the driver what it was.

As soon as I found out, my husband and I immediately got on. What a ride! This 100+ year old cable car (looks just like the ones in San Francisco) kept going so uphill that in few minutes we were already out of the city and continued for about 20 minutes over a wooded area with trees and the like. Opicina was the last stop, but we were told to get off at the stop just before, the one that has an obelisk next to it. Why did we jump on the cable car? To see the amazing panorama from a high point of Trieste, the coast, and the bay. Remember, Opicina!

Another stunning site not to be missed in Trieste well, it is actually not in Trieste! Very close though, less than 6 miles from it. Is the wonderful Castello Miramare. A truly beautiful, classy, elegant castle built on the edge of the coastline overlooking the sea. Commissioned and built in 1850 by the Archduke Ferdinando Massimiliano of Asburg to become his and his dear Carlotta's residence. Miramare Castle never became the couple's love nest because he was killed in Mexico and Carlotta moved to Belgium. The different décor of the castle, Medieval, Gothic and Renaissance, blend elegantly, and the Archduke's passion for gardening can still be savored at the adjacent Miramare Garden.

Trieste has more to show to the attentive tourists who choose to visit it, also from a leisure point of view. It has museums, parks, boat rides that can keep you entertained for a while.

Or if you'd rather to do...nothing, you could too. But with style! Why not sit at the historic café's loved by the Triestini, well-known writers and poets of the past like Svevo, Saba, or Stendhal. Few of them to choose from, Caffe' degli Specchi in Piazza Unita', or caffe' San Marco or Caffe' Tommaseo, the oldest in Trieste, opened in 1830.

Having a caffe' or a cup of tea with a dolcetto (small pastry) in an elegant, historical café' is a great way to enjoy…. "nothing"! By the way, on a coffee topic, have you heard of ILLY caffe' brand? From Trieste.

Genova

What is the first thing that comes to mind if you think of Genoa? That it is the birthplace of Christopher Columbus? Or that Genoa is the largest port city in Italy? Maybe it is a world-famous signature dish, the delicious pasta with pesto Genovese? All these claims are true, but one thing I have noticed is that among foreign travelers, Genoa is not well known for its art, culture and incredible architecture. It is not for nothing that Genoa is nicknamed La Superba "the Superb". Let me tell you about it.

Nestled between the sea and the mountain, in Genoa it is possible to see the snow-capped mountains with your feet on the beach. And it is a city rich in history, a city full of contrasts, with the largest downtown and historic district in Europe, and alleys (here called carrugi) that are so narrow one can barely walk through them. At times, walking through these tiny alleys an unexpected scene opens before you, with grandiose buildings, or colorful and small humble ones. Imposing churches and monuments in the maze of the tiny alleys. Genova, with its 32 Mediaeval doors to enter the city, and the longest city walls in the world, after the Chinese Walls.

This is Genova, La Superba. Petrarca, the 13th century Tuscan poet, after visiting Genova described it with admiration saying "Genova, the regal city, Superb for men and walls, the Lady of the sea..." Let's take a look at some of Genova's landmarks.
La Lanterna, The Lantern, probably the most important symbol of the city for its citizen. Built in 1128, it is the third oldest lighthouse in the world still in operation. After climbing its 172 steps you will find yourself at the top to enjoy an extraordinary view of the city and its harbor.
Piazza De Ferrari (De Ferrari Square). Genoa's main square is named after Raffaele De Ferrari, the city's philanthropist. The square is overlooked by historical buildings such as Palazzo Ducale, (Doge's Palace) built in the 13th century. Impressive in its decorative details, it is now a museum.
Palazzo della Nuova Borsa (The New Stock Exchange Palazzo) built in 1912 is a great example of Liberty style at its best. I Palazzi dei Rolli (Dei Rolli Palaces) are sumptuous residences of the Genoese nobility.

These prestigious places can be found in various areas of the city, but especially in via Garibaldi e via Balbi. Via Garibaldi is listed as a UNESCO World Heritage Sites for its impressive architectural wealth. It is named after the Italian general Giuseppe Garibaldi. In addition to the Palazzi Rolli, on this street are the Palazzo Rosso e Palazzo Bianco (Red Palace and White Palace) other palaces owned by the noble family. Inside these palaces decorated with precious furnishing, they house important 16th century collections by Caravaggio and Van Dyck.

My favorite building in Genova is undoubtedly the Royal Palace. This very impressive palace built in 1618 is majestic in its proportions and a feast for the eyes of architecture lovers. As incredible as its façade is, its interior is even more captivating. It exudes class even in the smallest details. Genoa is deeply connected to the water, to the sea and naturally, many recreational activities are built near the sea and with the sea in mind. The Sea Aquarium is the #1 attraction in Genova with over 1 million visitors each year and the 2nd largest aquarium in Europe after the one in Valencia. Not only children, but adults also will enjoy it (I did). A few feet away from the Aquarium, if you want to see an extraordinary 360 degrees view of the city, mountains, harbor and bay, you can (for a fee). A transparent elevator will climb high enough for you to enjoy this spectacular view.

If you are more interested in nature, you can learn about the delicate ecosystem of flora and fauna at the Biosphere, a large, very scenic spherical structure in steel and glass, bubbles of water enclosing tropical vegetation inside. The Biosphere is also located near the Aquarium.

Before leaving Genova another place that I really enjoyed visiting, was the village of Boccadasse. Arriving there it seems like time has stopped. Boccadasse looks like is coming out of a painting of a mariner's village, with the fishermen's boats anchored by the shore and the old colorful houses surrounding it. So beautiful and characteristic.

Bologna

The largest and most important city in Emilia Romagna region, rises at the center of the Po' Valley (the Po' is the largest river in Italy). This is the city where history, culture, and its deep passion for food, blend so harmoniously down to the soul of this vibrant city, making a visit to Bologna a complete experience even for a savvy traveler.

Bologna has roots that can be traced back to the 6th century B.C. being an important Etruscan city of that time. Under many ancient Bolognese houses of Medieval structure, you can still find the foundation of this Roman city which dates to the 2nd century B.C. What is peculiar of this city is the way it has been affectionately nicknamed. Yes, another city with a nickname, and if Genoa has 1 nickname, "The Superb" that defines it, Bologna has even 3!

As I will go more into details, they are all very fitting to the city.

The first nickname with which Bologna has been called by for hundreds of years and it is certainly the one is most known for, is "La Dotta" meaning "The Learner", derived from the fact that it is an ancient university city. Bologna has been a center for learning since the 7th century. Its university, still called with its original Latin name, Alma Mater Studiorum, was founded in 1088 and has operated continuously ever since, holding the title of the oldest university in the world. The most famous and impressive monument in Bologna are the two iconic towers of the city. Built in Medieval architecture, Torre degli Asinelli

(321 feet) and Torre Garisenda (157 feet) were both built in the 1100s. The towers, in addition to giving prestige to the family's name that built it, served mainly as a military watchtower.

Have you ever wondered what it was like to live 1000 years ago? Wonder no more! No need to watch documentaries or movies sitting on you couch to have an idea. You can get the real feel. At the Asinelli tower.

How so? Just climb all 498 steps to the top of the Asinelli Tower and you will know how it feels like to live 1000 years ago. (When I climbed the steps to go to the top of the Leaning Tower of Pisa I had my real feel too, "only" 300 steps but on a much narrower space).

Now that you are at the top of the 300+ foot tall tower, you are rewarded with an incredible view of the entire city, which brings me to Bologna's 2nd nickname, "La Rossa" which means "The Red", referring to the red brick roofs of Bologna's buildings. By doing 1 thing (climbing the tower) you achieved 3 goals: you got a real feel of life 1000 years ago, you saw an amazing view of the city, and you got your exercise for the day. That is fantastic! Now let's go down 498 steps to continue with the main historical attractions of Bologna.

In addition to the two towers, the most representative landmark of Bologna and just 5-minute walk from the towers, is Piazza Maggiore (Major Square) Bologna's main square and one of the most ancient squares in Italy. Built in 1200, with its typical medieval style, Piazza Maggiore is the heart of Bologna. Four main buildings overlook this important and thriving square, Palazzo d'Accursio, it used to be the City Hall, now a museum. Palazzo dei Notai, the notary's Palace. Basilica di San Petronio, a massive church, the last one being built (starting in 1390) in Gothic style, is the fifth largest church in the world. Palazzo dei Banchi, a prestigious building once a banking center.

Piazza Maggiore is the place where all major events of the city take place and where the Bolognesi love to meet. A fun peculiarity you can find in this area is 4 cantoni del Podestà. Located by Palazzo Re Enzo, you will discover a unique and amusing phenomenon: the opposite corners can "communicate" with each other. Whisper into one corner and your friend can hear every word you say from the opposite corner! Today the call it "the cordless phone". (Speaking of peculiarity, La Finestrella - the little window- in via Piella, is also worth a stop).

In the nearby Piazza del Nettuno, it is certainly worth taking a look even if only for a few photos, at the interesting structure of the building, full of arches on every floor, the Biblioteca Salaborsa (Salaborsa library).

Palazzo dell'Archiginnasio. This is the most beautiful building in Bologna. Usually, the hasty tourist passes quickly by the front door throwing only a distracted glance at the central portico, but not the savvy one, the savvy tourist savors every moment, and just by looking up for a moment would be amazed by the long portico with 30 arches and hundreds of coats of arms that beautifully cover the ceiling. This Palace was a place for teaching until 1838 when some changes were made to make way for the library.

The next two stops will make you feel like a local. Guaranteed by the locals who always frequent these beautiful and popular places for various reasons. Quadrilatero. (The Quadrilateral) This quadrangular -shaped area and historic district has housed most of the shops and markets since Middle Ages, is one of the most characteristic places in Bologna and a must-see when visiting the city. The four streets that make up the area are full of shops of all kinds. From luxury to mid-range boutiques, cafés or delicatessen, vegetables and fruits stall where locals shop, there is something for everyone.

Libreria Ambasciatori (and Eataly). This is another place where the locals love to hang out. The Ambasciatori Bookshop is a very interesting concept born in 2008: what was a large market in the 1800s is now a bookshop with a gourmet eatery, with the two beautifully arranged, blending together on three floors. In Bologna, the university city, you come to this bookshop, enjoy the intellectual atmosphere and eat! In a city so rich in food and culture, this place is where the two things marry together.

By the way, the 3rd nickname by which Bologna is also called is "La grassa", "The fat one". This one is quite self-explanatory, as the name tightly fits such a rich food flair and the belt...fits a bit tightly too after enjoying the rich food!

Ferrara

I was only 12 years old when I first went to Ferrara on a school trip, and the first thing that struck me was the incredible number of cyclists and bicycle stations (bikes parking) everywhere!

A multitude of bicycles instead of cars, people of all ages pedaling in the streets, squares, alleys, some stop for a minute in front of a shop to glance at the window, others simply to sit on a bench, that scene was just so nice to look at and it made such an impression on me, I remember thinking, "I want to move to Ferrara!" I also thought if the locals use their bikes in their daily activities, a visitor should too! The teacher did not feel the same way.

A tourist could and should do the same while visiting Ferrara, rent a bicycle for the day, mingle with the population. A fun and different way to see the sites, and certainly offers a deeper connection to the city's lifestyle. Ferrara is about 50 miles from Bologna, a few miles from the Adriatic Sea. It's a lovely town and very manageable to getting around all its areas on foot, by bus and, of course, people's favorite mean of transport, la bicicletta. Ferrara has walls all around the town like most of the ancient and historical towns, and like many old cities it has its own castle protecting it. The castle of Ferrara was another thing that made a huge impression on me: its mightiness in sight. Standing in the center of a large square, in 1385 the construction of the Castello d'Este began, commissioned and owned by the Este family, a princely family linked with other royal families in Europe.

Its medieval architecture gives it an austere but beautiful appearance. The castle also has a drawbridge, something unusual in a castle in the middle of the city. This powerful and fascinating castle is a must-see attraction even if you are in Bologna. Worth taking the short drive.

San Giorgio Cathedral. Another impressive building from an architectural standpoint. Built in 1135, this cathedral has with it a mix of different styles, starting from the Gothic façade and some Romanesque and Renaissance on the sides and interiors. Ferrara also has a shopping area, arcades, museums, a great food culture like everywhere in this region. Being not far from the sea, it makes it a perfect day trip from other locations to enjoy both the city and the sea, or better yet, stay there for the weekend.

Orvieto

The region of Umbria is a like a hidden jewel in the navel of Italy off the tourist trail. Beautiful countryside, lakes, and even the highest and most beautiful waterfall in Italy, Cascata delle Marmore, can be found in this small region. Quaint towns and villages full of history like Orvieto. This Etruscan town has many reasons to be visited.

The main landmark of Orvieto is its Duomo. It is so imposing in its size, height, and structure, I was literally amazed when I first saw it. Built in 1285, it is a splendid example of Italian Gothic architecture. This impressive cathedral, (you can see it from afar upon arriving in this town perched on a cliff) has a stunning façade, rich with gold mosaics throughout and decorated by the best artists of the time. The reflection of the sun on the mosaics gives it an incredible shine and adds splendor to this masterpiece of art.

Pozzo di San Patrizio, Well of Saint Patrick. Is the 2nd most important landmark and attraction in Orvieto after the Duomo. It was built in 1527 and is 203 feet deep. It was built with the aim of having enough water all year round in the event of calamity or a prolonged siege. It has a cylindrical shape and very interestingly, it can be visited, yes you can go to the bottom of it. The well was built with a staircase that allowed a man and an animal to go up and down,

and 72 windows that opened to let the light in almost till the bottom of it. What a work of engineering for those days!
The Well can be visited, and if you wonder how it feels like to live 500 years ago... you know what to do! Just think, the 498 steps of the Asinelli Tower in Bologna versus only 248 at St. Patrick's Well. I will not say it's a walk in the park, but for sure, it's a walk in the Well!

If you like archeology and exploration, you can do both in Orvieto: it is called Orvieto Underground. This quaint town not only is stunning above the ground but equally interesting below it.
That is what Orvieto Underground is: an underground town, with tunnels (more than a thousand of them) 2500 years old, from the Etruscans to the Renaissance. For more info visit www.orvietounderground.it

Orvieto is also very charming to stroll through its ancient streets typical of the Middle Ages, with narrow alleys that suddenly open onto squares, churches, towers, arches, artisan shops and local eateries. There is so much to see, do and enjoy in such a small town. Umbria is a jewel, and Orvieto is one of its most precious gems. A sweet sidenote about Umbria: the famous, delicious chocolate truffle Baci Perugina with its love notes written in many languages comes from Perugia, the capital of Umbria.

Caserta

Caserta is a town in the Campania region less than 1 hour north of Naples. Caserta, like many towns, has its old quarter, but unlike most other towns and cities, in which the old quarter is within the city itself, Caserta Vecchia (Old Caserta) is about a 15-minute drive from the town and uphill.
Old Caserta is a very charming Medieval village, with its castle, cobblestones alleys, houses decorated with plants and flowers, souvenir shops, restaurants with typical regional dishes.

I recommend visiting Old Caserta in the late afternoon and then ending the day with a nice dinner at one of the local eateries. Why in the afternoon, you may ask? Because first you should start and spend the day in another place that Caserta is very famous for.
Although old Caserta is charming, what makes Caserta world known for, is its majestic, and never a word has been more appropriate to describe it, majestic Reggia di Caserta. The Royal Palace of Caserta. Yes, this small town is home to a king's Palace. Seeing it from afar, the Royal Palace is absolutely spectacular.

The King Borbone of the Royal dynasty of Naples, already residing at the Royal Palace in Naples, (see page 31, the Palace with the most incredible views of Naples, the bay, the garden, and Vesuvio) had the Royal Palace of Caserta built as a summer residence. He wanted to create an imposing structure that could rival the Palace of Versailles in grandeur.
Et voila' madames and messieurs, King Borbone certainly succeeded in his intent, which obviously also meant more international prestige for his name. First stone was set in 1752 and completed in 1774, this marvelous masterpiece of architecture is the largest royal residence in the world in size. Just the palace itself alone is 47000 square meters or 506000 square feet.
The Palace features sumptuous interiors, impressive stairways, high ceilings with precious frescos, notable paintings, an Opera House, and the Royal private apartments. Make sure you do not miss the room of the Queen Maria Carolina, la stanza degli specchi (the room of mirrors) with sumptuous Venetian Rococo' mirrors.

As stunning as the Palace is everywhere you go, in the outdoor spaces it is where its grandeur shows itself on a monumental scale. The Royal Park is inspired by the Park of Versailles but regarded as superior in beauty. The Park starts from the back of the façade of the Palace, flanking a long avenue of fountains and waterfalls.
It combines the tradition of the Italian Renaissance Garden, whose peculiarity is the geometric subdivision of the spaces through trees and evergreen bushes, architectural elements such as fountains and statues to the pleasure of the view of the garden, merged with the English garden, a landscaped garden style that mimics nature in its waterways, lakes, grottos.
The result of these two styles used to create the Park is a mesmerizing masterpiece. More so if the Palace and Park are seen from an ariel view: the entire property has the shape of a violin. How ingenious!
I remember once I read "not visiting the Royal Palace of Caserta is an attack on world culture". The site is part of the Unesco World Heritage Site. Absolutely a must see.

To visit the Royal Palace of Caserta I suggest you reserve the whole day to enjoy it to the fullest. Very easy to reach especially by train. Get off at Caserta station and the Reggia is in front of you.
A lot of walking is involved to visit both the Palace and its Park. In case long walks are not your favorite thing, no worries, there is a bus that runs through the park, or if you will be feeling a little more regal that day, a horse -drawn carriage will be waiting for you (for a fee).

Fun facts about la Reggia di Caserta:
-If you like numbers the Palace has 1200 rooms, 1026 fireplaces, 1742 windows, 56 stairways, 1 chairlift (it was a kind of elevator built for the king).
-Above the splendid staircase of honor, a little secret "trick" was hidden. In the frescoed dome there is a space made for a small orchestra, not visible to passers-by, which played gracious melodies to welcome the king when he entered the palace.
-In 1861 officials of the Savoy King visited the Palace and found something that looked odd to them. Not understanding what it was, they listed it as "strange object shaped like a guitar". The object was a bidet.
-The Royal Palace of Caserta was chosen as film location for movies and tv series. Among them "Mission Impossible III", Star Wars in the episodes "The phantom Menace" and "Attack of the Clones", where some of the interiors of the Palace were used to represent the palace of the planet Naboo. I have to say, I would have never guessed that one, but then again, I am one of the about 20 people on the planet (Earth) who have never watched Star Wars...

Alberobello

There is not another place in the world like Alberobello and is not for its monuments (there are none), not for its castles (no castles there), neither for its artistic fountains (not even one) so, what makes Alberobello special, charming, and unique? Its houses. To be precise, cone shaped houses. All cylindrical, all with a cone roof, all white and grey. All amazing. And a Unesco World Heritage location.
Located in Puglia region, not too far from Bari, Alberobello, (Beautiful-tree), is a village of about 10,000 inhabitants. The shape of the houses called trulli, made Alberobello a renowned tourist destination. The first record of a settlement and trulli being built goes back to the 14th century. Due to some feuds between the Lords of the time, the houses were built using drywall and limestone, to be easily dismantled by the Lord's order to evade taxes on the houses. Trulli are still there for the world to enjoy. I visited Alberobello a few years ago, I enjoyed wandering aimlessly as, on occasions, it is the best way to get the feeling of a new place, where a surprise awaits you around the corner. Alberobello surprised me many times with something to photograph, and the plants with colorful f.lowers along with the white of the houses, completed the beauty of the place. Some souvenir shops allow you to go on the terrace, I did and took pictures of the roofs of the houses, such an interesting and pretty sight. Some trulli are also open to the public to get an idea how they furnished the interior given the unusual round shape of the house, so utterly cute!

Palermo

This eclectic city, at the crossroad between the Mediterranean and Northern Europe, has been said to be most conquered city in the world in 3 Millennia. Founded in 734 B.C. and called Ziz (sounds quite different from Palermo!), even the food is a melting pot of flavors from every era: Phoenician, Greek, Carthaginian, Roman, Gothic, Byzantine, Arab, Norman, Swabian, Angevin and Aragon.

There are numerous monuments and interesting places that make this city a tourist destination and an excellent starting point (especially if you arrive by plane) to visit the beautiful island of Sicily. Just to name a couple, the Teatro Politeama Garibaldi is an impressive building with a triumphal arch and a large bronze statue on top of it, arches all around on both two floors of its exterior facade. Built in in 1865 in one of Palermo's main squares, it is reminiscent of Greek and Roman architecture.

At night is when the building looks its best with the lights pinpointing the building's features, and when you can also enjoy a beautiful evening in this Opera House that hosts the Sicilian Symphony Orchestra.

It does not end here, because Palermo has not one, but two Opera Houses. The Teatro Massimo Vittorio Emanuele, built only a few years after the Politeama, whose construction started in 1874, is larger than its competitor and located just a few squares from it. With typical Greek style columns at the entrance and a dome, this grand Opera house is at its best inside, as the exceptional acoustic of Massimo Opera House are world-renowned.

Speaking of acoustics, a totally different kind of acoustic occurs every morning less than 10-minute walk of the Massimo Opera House. The Vucciria, a local (and vocal!) flea market, is very famous for its multitude of stalls of all kinds flanked by owners yelling over each other trying to get the customer's attention. In addition, to finding great bargains on produce, clothes, gadgets and so on (I can proudly say I did!), it can be fun to hear all these voices yelling in their typical Palermitano accent.

If you have a day to spare, or even less, just from early afternoon to evening (I'll say more about this a few lines down) and depending on whether you are more interested in culture and art, or if you are more of a beach person, there are two very famous and appealing destinations just outside of Palermo that I recommend you don't miss. Monreale and Mondello.

Monreale is a town about 8 miles from the center of Palermo located in a hilly area at the foot of Mount Caputo overlooking a valley that reaches the sea. The Cathedral of this ancient village is what Monreale is most famous for.

Construction began in 1174 and was completed in just 4 years, this imposing structure it's a great example of Norman architecture.

The Normans chose Monreale as their base town to live in after going to battles. Really nice to stroll through the small streets of this quaint village.

Another reason why you should visit Monreale is its location. Being at 310 meter above sea level (about 1000 feet) it offers an incredible view of the city of Palermo, the valley surrounding it and, of course the beautiful sea.

The sea. This brings me to the 2nd destination, you absolutely should not miss (when I am in Palermo I certainly don't), Mondello, which is about 10 miles from Palermo. The beach of Mondello is simply incredible! White sandy beach and crystal-clear waters, you will feel like you are in the Caribbean.

Amazing scenery all around, Mondello is not just a beach, it is a beautiful residential area, with a garden surrounded by greenery near the beach, bars and restaurants, many shops on the waterfront for a nice walk and, as icing on the cake, the historic and celebrated restaurant on the pier.

This classy restaurant, (for several decades it was called Charleston, recently "Alle Terrazze") opened in 1913, was decorated in Liberty style so in vogue a century ago, both in the structure of the building and in the interior. It was "the place" where officials, affluent people and even the Savoy Royals had dined. It has changed ownership a few times during the more than 100 years since it opened, but what has not changed is the elegance of the setting and in the presentation of their dishes.

After visiting Monreale and enjoying the afternoon of diving into the turquoise waters of Mondello beach, if you want to indulge in sophisticated dining with the perfect ambience of sitting in this exclusive location on the pier overlooking the sea, moonlight as part of the décor on a beautiful summer evening, this is the place for you. Oh, what a beautiful and memorable day!

Cefalu' and Santo Stefano di Camastra

These two towns (30 min by train from each other) on the northern coast of Sicily are worth a visit for 2 different reasons I will list separately: Cefalu' is a famous resort place and a haven of tranquility at the same time.

You will enjoy walking around the narrow streets of this old town, the imposing cathedral built in 1131 AD located in the main and lively square, and the Lavatoio, a Saracen wash house, are the main tourist attractions of this charming town, as well as its sandy beach, from which you can enjoy a view of the town with its enormous rock behind it.

Santo Stefano di Camastra, a village by the sea, is <u>definitely worth</u> a visit for a very important reason: my parents were born there! What, you do not think that's reason enough to go to Santo Stefano? I really thought it was... what if I told you that Santo Stefano is the capital of ceramics? Practically everywhere on the main street you can see colorful shops with thousands of different types of ceramics in every possible style, from large ornamental ones to small and sometimes hilarious souvenirs.

There is an interesting museum of ceramics, and in the two main squares from which you can admire beautiful views of the sea, you will also notice ceramic tiles on the ground and on the railings. Ceramic is so important in Santo Stefano, the only high school there is, is a trade school that teaches you how to be an expert in creating any ceramic ornaments. There are ceramic factories of course, even my father as a teenager worked in a ceramic factory... what, my father working at the factory does not interest you? Ok, I promise, nothing more about my parents!

Seriously, if you happen to go to St. Stefano and you have a car, from there I also recommend going to Letto Santo, (Holy Bed) where in about a 20-minute drive, less than 10 miles, you go from sea level to 3,000 feet height. The road ends when you get to the church at the top. All you have to do is to park your car and enjoy incredible views of the landscape around you, the pretty houses here and there and the sea far in the distance.

On the way back, if you are getting hungry, the mountain does that, I suggest a stop at Ritrovo Felicita, a restaurant with a terrace overlooking the beautiful landscape, but you will feel like you are at a friend's house. The owners are attentive and friendly, they only serve local and seasonal produce, and the dishes are just mouthwatering. Their appetizers and pastas with eggplant or pancetta and pistacchio are customers' favorites.

After such a delicious meal it is time for a dessert. If you love pistachios, try their amazing pistacchio lava dessert, to be savored slowly to fully enjoy its flavor and texture. Felicita is one of my favorite restaurants to go to. In Santo Stefano there is also my favorite pastry shop, Bar Franco. The most delicious pastarella alla frutta, a short crust fruit pastry with the richest custard cream.

Taormina

The first thing that comes to mind when I think of Taormina, is a small jewel of inestimable value. As soon as you arrive you can almost feel the mythical atmosphere that has enchanted visitors from all over the world for hundreds of years. Positioned on a hill of Mount Tauro, the town of Taormina overlooks two enchanting bays below, and on the southern slope the summit of Mount

Etna with its volcano, often covered in snow during the winter, offering visitors a truly breathtaking and unforgettable view.

If you love history, archeology, art, great food, entertainment, shopping, the mountains (and there, is not just a "normal" mountain, but the highest and still active volcano in Europe) and, of course, beautiful beaches and crystal-clear water, all "packaged" in an elegant and unique place, you must visit Taormina. The remains of its Greek and Roman past are visible through the ruins of its castle and the medieval area.

The Greek theater, built in the 3rd century BC and later renovated by the Romans, is now used for summer performances. It has excellent acoustic and spectacular views of the sea and Mt. Etna.

The picturesque medieval area with the clock tower gate is a starting point for a walk through the old narrow streets and artisan shops. Piazza del Duomo has at its center a baroque fountain of a centaur (symbol of Taormina), and the church of San Nicola built in 1400, with pink marble columns.

Corso Umberto is the main street always very lively that will take you to piazza IX Aprile, the main square in Taormina. From this very spacious square with a large terrace, you can enjoy amazing views over the bay, Giardini Naxos and Isola bella (Beautiful Island).

In Giardini Naxos you can take boat trips, rent a scooter to move around or go up to Taormina. There are tours to Mt. Etna or to Catania, or even tours to the nearby Gole dell'Alcantara, the Alcantara Gorge. It is like going into a canyon by the sea!

A stay in Taormina should be at least 3 days, there is so much to see and do. Stroll through the side alleys, take your time, as they say "smell the roses" not only to see what is around, but looking at it, capture the moments. Sit in the piazza or wherever catches your curiosity, look around for a few minutes, feel the breeze or listen to the chatter in different language of the many who pass by from all over the world. Take some time to have a look at the different restaurants before choosing one, look at both the ambience and the menu' to sample some local or unusual recipes that inspire you and... buona serata!

Siracusa

I went to Siracusa years ago without doing any "homework" so to speak, without looking into to see what was there. I just booked the hotel in an historic area called Ortigia. No idea, no expectations. After getting off the train and wandering around Siracusa for a little bit, visiting the city and looking at the beautiful scenery, we headed to Ortigia. What a surprise and discovery! I could not get over how charming Ortigia was. Attached to the mainland by a short bridge, Ortigia is the oldest and the most fascinating area of Syracuse. Lovely to walk through the narrow streets and get lost in them.

As I write about Ortigia my mind and memories return to the time when I visited it, imagining myself wandering aimlessly on a summer night and the next morning when I was doing more sightseeing. As I am imagining the area and I am ready to describe what I saw, where I saw it, an Hamletian doubt suddenly comes to me: should I or should I not?

Would it be better for the reader to share everything I know or is it perhaps better to discover Ortigia as I did, blissfully clueless? It is clear to you that I liked it very much. Now I know.

For once, I think this is exactly what I' am going to do. Nothing. If you decide to go to Siracusa and Ortigia you should do the same! Don't search the internet to learn about this place. Just have fun going, seeing, living, and then.. leaving!

After you finish your freestyle tour of beautiful Siracusa, a suggestion on where you might go next: if you have time, after leaving Syracuse, go a little further south, about 35 miles from Syracuse is the small fishing village of Marzamemi. This delightful village where time seems to have stopped, not only has very characteristic alleys perfect for walking, but from the marina you can also admire a large rock or a tiny islet, with a beautiful villa on it, what a suggestive view!

Three or four miles south of Marzamemi there is the town of Pachino. Maybe this name sounds familiar to you even if you have never heard of this town? Most likely what sounds familiar is the word pachino: the famous Pachino cherry tomatoes grown in this area. This genuine and delicious Pachino IGP (indicazione geografica protetta – protected geographical indication) tomato has been recognized as a Unesco heritage. Grab a handful and try them: so juicy and flavorful, you will keep eat them one after the other, just like cherries...tomatoes!

Pachino is also the meeting point between the Ionian and the Mediterranean Sea. Two or three miles down the road, on another islet or large rock at a stone's throw from the mainland called Isola delle Correnti, there is a small monument with a plaque where it is written that you have reached the southernmost point of Sicily and Italy (not counting the small satellite islands). The spectacular view of the area definitely repays the whole journey to get there. So, relax and enjoy your day at the beach, you've earned it!

TUSCANY

Since I moved to America, over the years while conversating about Italy, I have noticed on many occasions that Americans are particularly fond of Tuscany. I can understand why, Tuscany is really one of a kind. Starting with its beautiful and varied landscapes, the countryside with rolling hills, the imposing Apennines, and the coastline. Its many cities are full of history and art, and the small villages so charming that they seem to come straight out of a storybook. Tuscany is known for its famous staple dishes like bistecca alla Fiorentina, the Florentine steak to name one, and above all its great wine tradition. This is the land of the world-famous Chianti wine, which comes from the town of Chianti, in the beautiful Chianti Valley. If you are planning a trip to Tuscany and would like to enjoy a night of excellent wine tasting, Chianti is the place to immerse yourself in the world of the expertise of Chianti wines matched with some traditional Tuscan dishes. Many also take classes, there are places that do both, cooking classes and wine tasting. Spending a few days in the Chianti area is a great way to blend the wine and food experience with the relaxation of the countryside, sipping some good wine over a good meal and watching the rolling hills at sunset, how beautiful! Of course, do some sightseeing in the nearby towns and villages. Tuscany has so many interesting and charming towns besides Florence that it would take at least a full week to visit them.

Pisa. If I think of one of a kind and Tuscany, Pisa immediately comes to mind. The (one of a kind) Leaning Tower, famous all over the world with the Cathedral and the Baptistry, both located in the beautiful and huge Piazza dei Miracoli (Miracle's Square) are impressive monuments of extraordinary beauty. Both were built around 1100 AD in Romanesque style. The cylindrical shape of the Torre di Pisa (Tower of Pisa) with its column all around on each of its 6 floors, gives the tower an unusual and elegant appearance to the tower so different from all the other square towers of the time and later, therefore the leaning part has certainly made this tower truly unique and known all over the world. The tower was not built with a slope. When it started to slightly lean on one side it was due to a structural subsidence of the ground.
I went to Pisa to see the tower on the last day it was open to the public to go to the top (it was closed for a while for a major restructure at the base to prevent further leaning) The 300 spiral staircase steps to climb were steep, little room to move and a bit tiring, but wow, what an amazing view from the top, it was worth the climb! The Leaning Tower of Pisa is a must see in Tuscany. Pisa is not just the Leaning Tower, there is much more art and history to see.

Lucca. Another lovely ancient town, one of my favorites in Tuscany, with an incredible history to admire wherever you walk, right from the entrance, through Lucca 's Medieval walls that surround the whole town. What is even more interesting about the walls is that you can visit around, above and inside! Intriguing to visit it with its tunnels and interior rooms. A historical landmark not to be missed is the Torre di Guinigi, (Guinigi's Tower). The tower, built in 1400 by the powerful Guinigi family in typical medieval architecture, has a peculiarity. If you climb its 230 steps (a breeze compared to the 500 in Bologna and 300 in Pisa) to get to the top, you will be rewarded by the amazing view of the old town of Lucca and its hills surrounded by trees and a garden. Yes, at the top of the tower there is a hanging garden which is several hundred years old! The reason? For the Guinigi family planting a garden on top of their tower was a way to stand out from all the other towers, and a rebirth for the town.

Pistoia. Halfway between Florence and Lucca, this pleasant old town is rich in art and history. Piazza del Duomo with the impressive San Zeno Cathedral, built in the 10th century, are the main landmark of the town and the starting point for strolling through the ancient and suggestive alleys and arcades.

Arezzo. What is particularly fascinating in Arezzo is its main square, Piazza Grande. One of the most beautiful and evocative squares in Italy. The square is not flat but goes downhill or uphill depending on where you come from. This medieval piazza has the typical buildings and tower of the time, but it is during the Renaissance era that it reached its peak of beauty with the addition of the Palazzo delle Logge.

Siena. Piazza del Campo is the iconic landmark of Siena. This beautiful, large square built in the Middle Ages is shell shaped with historic buildings around it. This piazza is world famous for the Palio di Siena, a horse race dating back to the mediaeval period, which is held in Piazza del Campo twice a year. The famous, imposing Duomo in Typical Romanesque - Gothic style is nearby. A great piece of architecture is The Palazzo Pubblico di Siena (or Palazzo Comunale). Built in 1288, it has a tower with a "crown" on top, grand interior façade, walls with descriptive paintings, vaulted ceiling all in Gothic style, it is impressive, worth a visit. It has always been the seat of the local Government.

San Gimignano. This village in the outskirts of Siena is my favorite village in Tuscany. Small but lovely, with much character and history. San Gimignano is a walled hilltop village surrounded by the beautiful Tuscan countryside built in the 3rd century, famous for its medieval architecture and its numerous towers, which can be seen miles away from the village. Entering this village is like stepping back in time, truly fascinating. Great wine tasting too.

Grosseto. Grosseto is perhaps less renowned among the famous cities of Tuscany, but its historic center is rich in cultural heritage and is certainly worth visiting. Enclosed by imposing walls, this town is not very large and is easy to visit. Piazza Dante is the main square surrounded by splendid colored palaces with arcades, and nearby is the Duomo di Grosseto. The cathedral, one of the landmarks of Grosseto, was built in 1294. From there stroll through the cobbled streets of the center dominated by the impressive Medici Fortress, from where you can see the town and the beautiful valley.
From Grosseto there are two very different locations perfect for day trips. Just 30 miles away is Orbetello, a charming old town that is well worth a visit. It overlooks a beautiful lagoon attached by a small strip of land to the Argentario promontory with its two quaint and a bit glam, seaside villages of Porto Santo Stefano and Porto Ercole. The other place not to be missed (especially for wellness lovers) 1 hour south of Grosseto are the thermal baths of Saturnia. The famous natural springs made of several natural pools of the Cascata del Mulino, a small waterfall of hot sulfurous thermal water, is not only beneficial for the skin, but is also a beautiful scenic site. Bring a bathing suit!

Isola d'Elba. (Elba Island). The largest island in the region, it takes 1 hour to reach it from the charming ancient town of Piombino. Elba is a picturesque resort destination, with many beautiful beaches, turquoise sea, and lovely villages. Portoferraio is the main and largest, followed by Campo nell'Elba, Capoliveri, Marciana, Porto Azzurro, Rio Marina and Rio nell'Elba, for a total of a just over 30,000 which increases considerably during the summer.
If you want to combine leisure time with history, in Portoferraio there several sites you can visit, from Napoleon's house to a museum with archeological finds dating back to the 5th century BC. If you like hiking, you can also do that. A great place to do this is a trail that takes you to the top of Monte Capanne. It is the highest peak on the island to reach, but once there you will be rewarded with an amazing view of the island, the Italian mainland, the French island of Corsica and the small islands of the Elba archipelago. Quite an experience to be able to see all of this from one place, isn't it?

Toscana, the one-of-a-kind region Americans are especially fond of, (probably the best-selling book and movie "Under the Tuscan sun" helped too!). By the way, the movie was shot in Cortona, another lovely Tuscan town worth seeing.

SEASIDE PLACES

Being a long peninsula surrounded for the most part by the sea with thousands of miles of coastline (many with spectacular views), big islands and numerous small ones, five months of warm climate, Italy is a great choice for a beach vacation. There are endless options of places to choose from as well as different ways to spend it. If your idea of vacation is relaxation on a secluded beach resort or endless entertainment and nightlife or anything in between, you will have plenty of choices that will suit your desires.

More often than not, when it comes to beach holidays, the place to spend them is chosen based on what one is looking for in terms of wants and needs from the type of holiday rather than the place itself. For this reason, in this new chapter I will describe locations and options not in geographical order, from north to south, but divided by categories. If you want to be in an exclusive environment, where should you go? What if you have a family with children? And what about campsites? Let's start this new tour, so pack your swimsuit and let's go to the beach!

What could be better than starting this seaside tour from an island famous for its incredible pristine waters, white sand beaches, an island whose sea is compared to the Caribbean? This island is also the most distant from the Italian mainland. This is **Sardegna.**
Since Sardinia is a very large island, there is a lot to see. The territory of the island is sometimes a bit harsh and wild, and this is part of its beauty. Sardinia is very famous for its wonderful beaches. Also, pink beaches. In the north of Sardinia, on the islet of Budelli, there is the splendid pink beach (the area is protected from an environmental point of view). The white and transparent sandy beach of Stintino, on the northern coast, is also very famous.

Santa Teresa di Gallura, located on an incredible bay and peninsula, is another resort destination renewed for its position, beach and amazing sea.
Not too far away, there are towns such as the charming **Alghero**, a town on the sea, and **Sassari**, not on the coast and more historic, making it a perfect stop for few days while touring Sardinia. They are close in distance but very different from each other, one modern and the other with ancient buildings, both interesting to visit. Even better, you could choose Santa Teresa, Alghero or Sassari as a base point and visit the other two as day trips for beaches or sightseeing the city. The wonderful islet (connected to the mainland) of

Sant'Antioco in the southwest of Sardinia, beautiful jagged rocks that form natural pools on the sea, white beaches and coves, a delightful village where you can spend your evenings tasting aperitifs and dinners in one of the typical Sardinian restaurants (make sure to try their typical bread, pane carasau and the seadas, the delicious ravioli stuffed with cheese, fried and covered with honey, what an intriguing combination, isn't it?).

On the eastern side of its southern tip is the capital of the island, **Cagliari**, a more modern city than all the others, but with very ancient origins. Historical monuments such as the Bastione di Sant Remy (bastion of Saint Remy), the cathedral Santa Maria from the 12th century in Gothic style, the beautiful Palazzo Civico a historical white palace with Gothic and Catalan elements, and of course the beautiful Poetto beach near the city, are the places not to be missed when visiting Cagliari. In this beautiful island there is a location that is the most celebrated of all, and when speaking of Sardinia, it is just impossible not to think of...

Top 3 luxurious resort areas: If you ask any Italian what the most exclusive, and posh seaside tourist destination in Italy is, where the rich and famous from all over the world love to spend their holidays, everyone will say....

Costa Smeralda. Yes, the number one luxury beach destination in Italy is Costa Smeralda (Emerald Coast) in the northern part of the beautiful island of Sardinia, and it truly lives up to its name. Pristine, crystal-clear waters, gorgeous white sand beaches (in some areas even the pink ones), incredible sceneries, all accompanied by top-notch service. Luxury hotels in secluded bays with private beaches, elegant restaurants with haute cuisine dining, shopping streets of exclusive brands, lively and picturesque piazzetta (square) with classy cafes to sip a cocktail or an aperitif at sunset, and glitzy clubs to end the night...in high end style, of course!

Not only are there 5-stars hotels at your fingertips, but you can also rent beautiful villas or even a yacht with captain, sailors and cooks at your disposal to take you where your heart desires. Porto Cervo, the main town in Costa Smeralda, was created to "complete" the natural beauty of the area with a structure capable of accommodating the sophisticated needs of the wealthy, the jet set from around the world can comfortably land almost in town with their private jets or dock in the harbor and are just minutes away from the famous piazzetta. Of course, there is also a wide choice of things to do during the day, from an excursion to the neighboring island of Corsica (once Italian, now part of France), or literally "diving" into all kinds of watersports, enjoying a massage on the beach and so on. The Costa Smeralda and its pretty towns with stunning beaches can be enjoyed not only by the rich and famous, but also by a large audience. On websites like Airbnb or Trivago, it is possible to find more affordable options for a vacation there, especially if you visit before or after July and August, the busiest season of the year.

Portofino. This picturesque mariner village and harbor in the Gulf of Liguria, is certainly one of the hotspots for high-class tourism on the Ligurian Riviera. The pastel-colored buildings all lined up on the shore, the beach, the yachts that line the harbor, its beautiful and famous piazzetta, a little gem perfectly embedded between the harbor and the cove where people gather to chat and sit at its elegant cafes, are just a few of the things that bring celebrities and artists from all over the world to Portofino and keep coming back to this corner of paradise. Still expensive, but less ostentatious than the Costa Smeralda. Even more historic. A hilltop fortress reachable via a panoramic walk from the village can be visited, offering stunning views of the gulf. Arriving to Portofino by boat is literally breathtaking.
Elite tourism chooses Portofino to admire its nature and for its charming but quieter atmosphere. When in Portofino a visit also to the nearby and lovely coastal towns of Rapallo, Santa Margherita Ligure and Chiavari is a must!

Capri. Oh Capri, Capri, Capri!! What hasn't already been said about this wonderful island? Well, one thing I am sure has not been said: I know a beautiful baby named after this island. A friend of mine recently had a baby girl, Capri'. Precisely for this reason I think baby Capri' should be given the citizenship of the Island of Capri!
Capri is probably the most famous and serenaded island in the world, and for many reasons: its breathtaking sceneries, the iconic Faraglioni, (3 gigantic, dramatic rocks just off the coast of the island), the Blue Grotto, the beautiful beaches and, of course, its two small towns, Capri and Anacapri, with their piazzetta full of restaurants, café' and world class shops.

Yes, Capri is famous for its postcard landscapes. The Faraglioni are certainly the most famous and photographed. It is interesting to note that the Faraglioni are not just huge rocks, each of them has a name, the closest to the mainland is Stella, next is di Mezzo (which is the one you cross by boat) and di Fuori. They can be admired from the beach or from the top of a promontory. From whatever angle you choose to look at them, they are absolutely jaw dropping!
La Grotta Azzurra, or The Blue Grotto is another famous and must-see gem of

this enchanting little island: the sunlight passes through this natural sea cave, giving its waters surprising reflections and brilliance to the delight of every tourist who goes to visit it. Experienced boatmen will take you to the cave to admire the different shades of blue of the water with the reflections of the sun. Capri is not only famous for its amazing scenery, but also for other things. Handmade leather and custom-made sandals are one of the things that Capri is known for. Have you ever wondered where Capri pants come from? Exactly. The location of the island of Capri is also spectacular, off the Gulf of Naples, close to Sorrento and the Sorrentine Peninsula, this small island is so unique, exclusive, celebrated in songs and films for countless years. Has attracted VIPs as far back as the time of the Roman Empire. The emperors loved Capri so much they spent their vacations and even retired there.

In modern times, Capri is home to celebrities from around the world who dock their yachts just off the coast for a glamourous vacation in this enchanting and sophisticated island, arriving in the evening to dine in one of its exquisite restaurants or to stay in one of the luxury hotels. The most famous and glamourous is the 5 stars Grand Hotel Quisisana. This grand hotel opened its doors in 1845 and it is very easy to find: right in the center of Capri, overlooking the most famous piazzetta on the island.

My favorite? "La Canzone del mare" hotel. The location is jaw dropping, near the Faraglioni rocks, which can be admired from afar from your hotel room. It has a beautiful private beach with crystalline turquoise water. The hotel is tastefully decorated, with the typical Capri majolica. The Diva suites, which take their name from the iconic divas of the 60s, are inspired by the furnishing style of those years.

As in the Costa Smeralda, Portofino and Capri are not just for the rich and famous and you do not have to spend a fortune to visit them. Moreover, due to the proximity and easy connection with other locations, Portofino and Capri can be visited in one day.

Costa Smeralda, Portofino and Capri have been Italy's top 3 most famous, luxurious, exclusive and distinctive seaside destinations for decades (Capri was already an elite tourism 2000 years ago as a privileged holiday resort of the Roman emperors).

Recently another island, a very small island about 3 miles long in southern Italy, has become known as the glamorous and chic hotspot for the rich and famous: **Panarea**. This Sicilian Island of about 250 inhabitants and part of the Aeolian islands group, is the destination of many jet set vacationers who, arriving aboard their yachts, choose it as the ideal place for their holidays, in

search of fabulous landscapes and beaches with a more secluded, laid-back atmosphere than Capri. Dropping the anchors in a beautiful bay, swimming in the southernmost part of the Tyrrhenian Sea, pleasantly strolling around the island and its beautiful village with upscale boutiques and restaurants and ending the evening in a relaxed and not overcrowded environment, is a great way to experience Panarea at its best in a nice and tranquil atmosphere (there is however an outdoor night club, in case some vacationers want to dance the night away!).
Of course, there are many other locations and upscale hotels that, while being more accessible in terms of price for a wider audience of tourists, offer their guests superior services and amenities for a pampered stay. From Capri these hotels can be found in nearby Sorrento and the Amalfi Coast.

Sorrento this lovely town situated on the tip of a hill overlooking the sea of the Sorrentine peninsula, not only offers breathtaking views of the bay and Capri, but has many charming, lively and colorful little streets full of shops, hotels with spa and everything your heart desires for a first-class vacation. By the way, have you ever had a sip of the famed Limoncello liqueur? If not, make sure to taste it right from where it was created, the romantic town of Sorrento. Lunch in Sorrento? Try the delicious linguine al limone (linguini with lemon), the famous and typical dish of the area... after taking a photo holding one of the huge lemons of Sorrento!

Near Sorrento, there are several small and charming villages along the Amalfi coast, *Amalfi, Positano* and *Ravello* being the most famous. All can be reached by land or by ferry from Naples or Sorrento. I would recommend the ferry; it would allow you to enjoy the best possible scenery of the coastline and the colorful, picturesque view of the towns cascading off the face of the mountains. From Naples, not only you can go to Capri, Sorrento and the Amalfi coast, but you can also visit Capri's two sister islands, Ischia and the smaller one, Procida.

Ischia. Despite being a much larger island than Capri, it was almost unknown as a tourist destination until the early 1950s, when Angelo Rizzoli, a publisher and film producer, went to Ischia with his yacht. He fell in love with the island and within a few years, he built hotels advertising them in his magazines, invited Hollywood stars of the 60s to the island, and this fishing island became a tourist destination (which has greatly helped the local economy) loved by many who spend their holidays here every year.
Ischia has several villages along the coast and in the center of it. They are all easily connected by local buses and mini (I mean really mini) taxi-cars. If you're

not too fussy about being super comfortable, the mini taxi can be a fun ride! Being a much bigger island with 6 small towns, a population of about 50,000 people, it is cheaper, with more tourist sites than its smaller and more famous sister island, Capri. You can easily spend several days in Ischia visiting its villages, doing excursions to places like Giardini La Mortella, Parco Termale Negombo, thermal gardens and beautiful beaches, enjoying every day.

The most important and impressive historical monument of Ischia is Castello Aragonese. The location of this castle is also incredible, built on a huge rock and connected to mainland via a small bridge. Ischia's landmark is quite an ancient one, being built in 474 B.C. During the late Middle Ages, in 1441 Alfonso D'Aragona built more buildings on this rock, turning it entirely into a fortified citadel. A couple of centuries later, about 2000 people lived there, which is very impressive, considering that it is a rock, huge, but still a rock. The Castello Aragonese is a picture-perfect spot, thanks to its location it allows to get excellent images from many angles, near or far. I have one I that I took long before the smartphone era, I used a disposable camera with the film inside (this is a quick trip down memory lane, who does not remember those cameras? Unless you were born after the year 2000, then you probably do not remember them or have never held one in your hand). The disposable camera photo turned out to be so beautiful that I enlarged and framed it on my living room wall to this day.

Hot Springs are another must in Ischia and one of the main things Ischia is known for. Since the time of the ancient Romans who traveled to Ischia to enjoy the beneficial effect of its thermal waters on health and skin. The most famous are the Giardini Termali Poseidone, Giardini di Afrodite and Giardini Tropicali just to name a few. Entrance (for a fee) to these parks allows you to choose natural pools of different water temperatures, saunas, paths as well as additional wellness services, mud treatments and of course, even a private beach. Among the 6 towns of Ischia my favorites are Porto, the largest where the ferry docks, a very lively town, and Sant'Angelo, chic and laid back, with breathtaking views.

Procida. This charming island with its beautiful pastel houses, high headland and amazing views, is the perfect place for a day trip.

Because it is so small and easy to get around, it doesn't take long to see the small town and scenic landscape, have lunch at one of the many restaurants, spend the afternoon on the beach swimming in its beautiful waters, and have time for one last stop at one of the harbor cafes for a local dessert before boarding the ferry to return to Pozzuoli or Naples. This is exactly what we did recently on one of my trips to Naples to visit my daughter and her husband. Although we went to Procida in mid-August, at the height of the busy summer season crowded with tourists around this small island, thanks to its relaxed atmosphere it never felt too crowded to be unpleasant, we had a lovely day there. Tip: check the ferry schedule in advance, there are only about 4 each way per day, so plan accordingly.

Continuing south towards Calabria, we find **Tropea,** a picturesque thousand-year-old village I always love visiting, known as the Pearl of the Tyrrhenian Sea. For good reasons. To name one, its position, with the houses reaching the edge of a cliff, a castle-shaped monastery built on the top of a huge rock with caves inside, give a very scenic presence to the whole area. The clifftop overlooking the crystal-clear waters of the sea with the beautiful white sand beach and the imposing rock nestled on the shore are an unforgettable sight. The lower part of the massive rock facing the sea offers curious visitors the opportunity to explore its two striking caves, both with a lovely sand beach. The Grotta del Palombaro is accessible by swimming or with a small boat. The other grotto called Grotta dello scoglio di San Leonardo aka Grotta delle Sirene (Mermaid's cave) is much easier to reach through stairs carved into the rock hundreds of years ago to limpid waters. Truly a one-of-a-kind place to visit. From the beach, reachable on foot and with a staircase of about 200 steps to climb, (with benches to sit and take pictures along the way) you can reach its downtown while also enjoying the breathtaking view of the small bay.

Tropea in 2021 was awarded as "il piu' bel borgo d'Italia" the most beautiful village in Italy. For many…. beautiful reasons. Tropea is not only a seaside place, but it also has much more to offer to the visitor who strolls the historic center of this charming village. Its ancient walls, narrow little streets and alleys, historic buildings, typical shops displaying local products, the numerous cafés' and restaurants to choose from, not to mention their famous cipolla rossa di Tropea (Tropea's signature sweet red onion) used in so many tasty dishes, they make it a great destination for families who want to combine natural beauties, amazing sceneries, history, art, and great food with the relaxed atmosphere of a southern coastal village. July and August are the busiest season, and the beaches are quite crowded while June and September are better choices if you prefer a more tranquil setting. Tropea being a small town does not have an airport. The closest is in Lamezia Terme, about 1 hour away with a well-connected train service from the airport to the town.
Speaking of beaches, one last thing worth noting about the beaches in Tropea; from there, looking out to sea, you will be able to see from afar the shape of

Stromboli, a volcanic island about 33 nautical miles from Tropea. Especially on a clear and sunny day, it is easy to notice the typical shape of the volcano (the longest still active in Italy) that, with a height of 900 meters or about 3000 feet, towers over the entire small island. A very suggestive view to look at while relaxing on the beach soaking up the sun.

The sunset over Stromboli as seen from Tropea is too beautiful and vibrant not to take the time to stop and miss it. Its intense yellow, orange and reddish colors settle on the sea horizon, with the cone shaped island completing the picture-perfect moment. If you go to Tropea, remember to watch the sunset!

Stromboli, which is about 33 nautical miles (about 60km) from Tropea, can be easily reached by a fast ferry in 1 ½ hour. This small island with a population of about 500 inhabitants is part of the Aeolian Islands, made up of 7 islands off the northern Sicilian coastline. Stromboli is the furthest, slightly closer to Calabria than to Sicily. It can certainly be a great and fun idea to take a day excursion to this Sicilian Island, adding more flavors (Sicilian ones) to your Calabrese vacation.

(As a side note, it always sounds a little strange to hear the word Stromboli in America referred to food. And as Italian food, which by the way, I've never seen anywhere in Italy. Stromboli for every Italian is the small island in the Mediterranean Sea. Stromboli for every American is a pizza-calzone. Ah, these amusing peculiarities of life...)

Going back to the Eolian Islands, I have already mentioned two of them, Panarea and Stromboli. The other five are *Vulcano, Salina, Alicudi, Filicudi* and the largest, *Lipari*.

This archipelago of tiny islands, all of volcanic origin (Vulcano and Stromboli are still active, in Stromboli is even possible to see the fumaroles coming out of its cone practically every day) give them a unique type of soil, flora and fauna. Some beaches are very dark due to the volcanos, with thermal waters and muds that are not only pleasant, but also beneficial for the skin.

The Aeolian Islands are a Unesco World Heritage Site and have been nicknamed the Hawaii of the Mediterranean. **Lipari**, being the largest and most populated, is certainly the island with the most to offer in terms of things to do and see also from the historical point of view, with several monument and even a castle. And what a castle.

The history of the castle area of Lipari dates back almost 4000 years and archaeological excavations have confirmed this. Its surrounding walls were completed around 500 AD. This imposing castle stands on a promontory overlooking the sea, up to 50 meters or 150 feet above sea level. From that point, amazing views of the town, port and sea are guaranteed. Chiostro Normanno di Lipari built in 1134 is another must-see when visiting the island. Marina Piccola, Lipari's lively downtown with a charming main square in the center, is the island's hot spot. Cafés, restaurants and shops are all around. Beautiful sandy or rocky beaches, as well as a white sand beach due to the nearby pumice quarry.

Not only in Capri you can admire the faraglioni, but also Lipari has its own faraglione and its nearby grottos. Finally, if you are also looking for some culture in Lipari, il Parco Archeologico Regionale delle Isole Eolie e Museo Luigi Bernabo' Bra (the Regional Archaeological Park of the Aeolian Island and Museo Luigi Bernabo' Bra) will certainly amuse you with its art crafts and give you the opportunity to learn about the interesting millennial history and geography of the island.
Lipari is an excellent starting point for visiting the other islands. The easiest and shortest way to reach the Aeolian Islands is from Milazzo, about 30 miles from the city of Messina, and choose between the ferry or the faster hydrofoil.

The intriguing island of **Vulcano**, with its numerous hiking trails to the top of the volcano, thermal baths and dark sandy beaches, is the perfect choice if you want to combine sport, physical well-being and comfortable recreation.
Salina is the 2nd largest island after Lipari and with a population of 2000 inhabitants, it is loved by the most experienced generations and by families with children thanks to the right mix of relaxation and comfort to entertain either the youngest ones or the young at heart. Both islands are very close to Lipari but in opposite directions, and from both you can reach Lipari in (almost) no time at all.
Filicudi and **Alicudi** are the wildest, quietest and most unspoiled islands of the Archipelago. If you are looking for seclusion, peace and being totally in touch with nature forgetting the world around you or far away from you, these two islands are the perfect solution for your long-awaited vacation.
Doesn't all this seem secluded or isolated enough? There is more: if the streetlights bother you, or the sound of a car engine annoys you, Alicudi will make you happy because there is neither. Although you might hear the braying of a donkey if you get on it... for transportation!

The Aeolians Islands are not the only Sicilian Islands. Mamma Sicilia has a few other small, enchanting islands under her large wings. One of these is **Ustica,** an island formed thousands and thousands of years ago, following a volcanic eruption whose traces can be seen on its dark land, is located about 40 miles north of the city of Palermo, which is the departing point to reach Ustica through its daily ferries and hydrofoils service. Known for its many beautiful grottos and caves that open along the high coastlines, as well as for the numerous rocks that surround the deep blue waters of the islands. Its submerged seabed full of life protected by a marine reserve in the name of biodiversity conservation, undoubtedly make Ustica an excellent destination for all scuba diving lovers.

Just off the west coast of Sicily, from the city of Trapani, with a short ferry ride (less than 10 miles from Sicily) you can reach Le isole Egadi, the Aegadian Islands. A group of tiny islands with **Favignana** being the largest and closest to the islands of **Levanzo,** so close you can clearly see it from afar, and **Marettimo**.
What is stands out about these islands is certainly its unspoiled wilderness, in stark contrast with its crystal-clear sea water and emerald color bays, hidden caves that open onto blue waters of different shades, the wild nature of the islands pair up with its equally wild beauty.
Being Favignana the largest, it certainly has more to offer to the visitor or to families looking for comfort and things to do, while Levanzo and Marettimo with their old fisherman villages, white house with colored doors, a population of only few hundred inhabitants, they are the ideal destination for those who want a quiet and relaxed atmosphere for their vacation. In Marettimo cars are not allowed, only local taxi to take guests from the port to their destination and few others are granted the permit to circulate on the island.
From Favignana it is possible to take a day trip to both Levanto and Marettimo, numerous small boat services are available to take you to both locations. Some of them even offer an organized full day excursion with tours with a typical Sicilian lunch is included. A website you can consult that is also translated into English is www.brezzamarinafavignana.com .

Trapani, while not very far from Palermo, also has its own airport which saves time (instead of flying into Palermo and taking a train or car to get to Trapani). One more thing: if you visit Trapani and the Isole Egadi, you can't miss **Erice**, a small and ancient town less than 30 minutes from Trapani. This historic and picturesque hilltop town is a must see if you are in the area...and even if you are not, it is worth the trip! Going further south between Sicily and Africa, closer to it, just 40 miles from the Tunisian coastline and over 50 miles from the nearest Sicilian coast, lays the foundation with its intriguing and unique flavors, the beautiful island of **Pantelleria**. This island, which is the largest of all the satellite islands belonging to Sicily, is the only one that is not part of an archipelago. Due to its geographical position, Pantelleria has its own biodiversity in terms of climate, soil, flora and fauna, with peculiarities that belong only to this island. It is no coincidence that Pantelleria has earned two nicknames, both suggestive, that well describe this fascinating place.

Pantelleria has been named Black Pearl of the Mediterranean, for its volcanic origins, the testimonies of which is visible in its lava rocks and in the soil of the whole island, and it is also called Figlia del Vento (Daughter of the Wind) for the breeze that never stops blowing.
Another peculiarity of the island, which is also one of its main tourist attractions, is lago Specchio di Venere, (Mirror of Venus Lake) so called because legend says that the goddess Venus was reflected in the lake before meeting Bacchus. This lake is such a beauty, a joy to behold even when looking at it from afar.
Of a beautiful bright light blue color, the lake sits on the crater of a volcano, right in the center of the island. The peculiarity of being in that place is what makes the lake even more famous: its thermal baths, pockets of ponds from which water at over 110 F comes out. Covering the body with thermal mud is known to have beneficial properties for the body, so tourists in addition to sunbathing and swimming in the beautiful water of this lake, they make sure to set aside time for an open air, one of a kind (and free) spa service!

In addition to the lake, there are many sites not to be missed in Pantelleria. The Arco dell'Elefante (the Arc of the Elephant) is a huge rock with the resemblance of the elephant's that trunk enters the sea creating a large arch shape. The Sesi are also one of the landmarks for which Pantelleria is known. They are megalithic constructions built about 5000 years ago. The term sese in Pantelleria is referred to a pile of stones. Being in the center of the crossroad of the Mediterranean Sea, Pantelleria has a lot of history to tell, a big castle can be seen when arriving at the port is part of that history, as well as an ancient acropolis.

Of course, being an island and being this chapter about seaside holidays, Pantelleria fits into anyone's wish list (couples, friends, families or even a solo trip) for a nice vacation.
Lots of beaches to sunbathe and relax, historical sites for some culture or just enjoying nature during its hot, dry and breezy summer and, of course, Italy is always about food, and food is always about tasting the typical dishes of the area you are visiting. On such small island, is there anything growing right from

there? Yes, there is! Actually, there are! Pantelleria is very famous for its capers, I capperi di Pantelleria, whose plants and pretty flowers find a very fertile soil, thanks to its volcanic roots. The locals are masters when it comes to using it in any type of dish to give it that special and flavorful touch (you will be surprised to see what a versatile and tasty ingredient capers are in so many recipes).

When it comes to wine, Pantelleria has its own special one, so special that since 2014 Unesco has granted world heritage status for the way it is cultivated. The type of wine is called Passito di Pantelleria, which derives from a type of grape that grows well in that type of soil and climate.

The locals turn the Passito into a local sweet wine, the zibibbo, a wine perfect to sip and taste at the end of a meal with a dessert, obviously local, and to complete the dinner wouldn't be nice to go back to your summer residence…like a local? You can, in a dammuso, an ancient building made of lava stone, so typical of the island.

Although Pantelleria is located south of Sicily near the African coast, there is another trio of very small islands even further south than Pantelleria, making it the southernmost tip of Italy between Malta and Tunisia, just 37 miles from the latter and 72 from Sicily. This is the archipelago of the Pelagie made up of three small islands.

Lampedusa with a population of 6000 inhabitants is the largest in size, a whopping 2 miles wide and about 8 miles long. The other 2 islands are **Linosa**, about 200 inhabitants, beautiful beaches, the charm of the laid-back lifestyle is perfect for those who love tranquility and nature on vacation or for a sight & sea day trip when in Lampedusa, and then there is **Lampione**, which is pretty much a huge rock with one teeny tiny road that will direct you to the only construction on the island, a lighthouse.

By the way, if love adventures there is one unique thing that you can do in Lampione, watch sharks! Yes, and you would be watching them in their environment, which means that you will be in the water too. This sounds like quite an experience you'll be able to tell your grandchildren about one day, or if you can't wait that long, friends are a perfect audience to brag about too!

Lampione is the only place in Europe where you can do this, so if you are in the area jump in, literally! You must be a certified scuba diver to jump, actually dive, into this quite unique experience. The website to book the scuba diving immersions, take scuba diving courses or simply book a ride or a full day tour from Lampedusa to Lampione and Linosa (here with lunch included on board) is the following: www.pelagoslampedusa.it

If you are not up for such a thrilling experience but still want to have fun in the sun, experiencing nature above and below the water, no worries, the Pelagie Islands are a natural paradise not only for experienced scuba divers, but also for novice snorkelers. Families might experience the added joy of seeing their children super excited (and us adults too!) at the sight of dolphins, fin whales or blue whales as they cruise by boat from site to site. For a few weeks during the summer, these huge mammals can be found in the open waters of the island's crystal blue sea.

Speaking of blue and crystalline waters, my mind immediately runs to the image of one of the most beautiful sites in the world, that of the Isola dei Conigli (Island of Rabbits) in Lampedusa. Upon reaching the area, the view from the top is simply breathtaking: looking at the contrast from the rugged land all around you suddenly encounter fine and white sandy beaches, different shades of turquoise glimpsed through the calm waters, the small islet (Isola dei Conigli) almost annexed to the main island, this pristine territory is one of unparalleled beauty that certainly deserved the title awarded in 2013 as the most beautiful beach in the world.
Interestingly, the Island of Rabbits should probably be renamed the Island of the Sea Turtles, in summer they all go there to lay their eggs at night, so the area has become a protected nature reserve, and the beach can only be visited during the day.
Isola dei Conigli is not the only wonderful beach on the island, Lampedusa is renowned for the extraordinary clarity of its sea, throughout the island there are bays that open onto inlets with rocky or white sand beaches. To mention a couple, la Tabaccara, near the Isola dei Conigli. Its waters are as transparent as being in a natural swimming pool, and especially when looking at the bay from the cliff above it seems as if the boats below are suspended in the air, so much so as to give the area the nickname of "the bay of the flying boats".

Cala Guitgia is another bay that opens to the splendid scenery typical of the island with its beach and clear waters. It is probably the most famous in terms of accessibility and services and therefore also the most popular and crowded in the months of July and August. It can be reached with a short walk from the city center of Lampedusa. Cala Guitgia is well organized with umbrellas and sunbeds that can be rented for the day with restaurants and shops nearby, making it the perfect beach to go to for families with children and for those who love the convenience of being in a seaside town with all comforts at hand without even taking a bus or renting a car to get around.
Speaking of cars, the most popular ones to rent on the island are the Citroen

Mehari. Old French open-top cars reminiscent of the old small Suzuki Jeeps, Mehari's are perfect for cruising around the island giving the feeling of being on an adventurous, undefeated paths and these open-air cars provide the natural breeze of driving on a summer day in... North African climate! To add to the adventurous feeling, Mehari is not like driving a normal car also because the gearbox is the one used in old French cars. It's a fun car, almost like a moving landmark there, and you will see many colorful ones around.
It definitely adds to the experience and uniqueness of a Lampedusa vacation. Of course, they also rent scooters, bikes and "regular" (mostly Fiat) cars. Here is a website for car rentals in Lampedusa www.noleggio-lampedusa.it

After having toured all the Sicilian islands let's go back to the mainland, precisely to the Puglia region on the "heel" of the Italian peninsula, for a stop in **Gallipoli**. The name of this ancient town gives a clear idea of why it should be visited. The name Gallipoli derives from the Greek words Kale Polis, which means beautiful city, an appropriate name for several reasons.
Its position is one of them: this town of about 20,000 inhabitants that stretches on the Ionian Sea is divided into 2 parts, the old town, which stands on an island connected to the mainland by a short and walkable bridge, and the more modern part of the city. The old town is fascinating, it seems almost a sort of small labyrinth with narrow winding streets and alleys, built in that way to protect it from the cold wind coming from the sea during the winter.

In the ancient town the most impressive monument that will catch your eyes for its size and its severe presence is the Castello Angioino Aragonese. This imposing medieval fortress almost surrounded by the sea, is the historical landmark of Gallipoli and is worth a visit.
During the summer however, it can only be visited from the outside as the highest part of the castle is used as an open-air cinema. The castle is located at the entrance to the old town (it makes perfect sense, to protect its inhabitants from potential invaders) just after the small bridge and is the starting point for visiting the narrow alleys that open to onto beautiful Baroque buildings. Strolling around, peaking at the small, cute shops and restaurants adds to the charm of Gallipoli, or Beautiful City. What Gallipoli is best known for, is its limpid sea that attracts tourists from all over. Hidden coves, the Mediterranean vegetation combined with the fine and clear sandy beaches, bring out the clarity of the waters even more. There are many pretty, beaches right at the entrance of the town, my favorite is about 6 miles from the center of Gallipoli where, at the end of a beautiful pine forest that opens onto an amazing bay, Spiaggia di Punta della Suina, with beautiful rocks and

sandy beach, lots of greenery, crystal clear sea and to top it off, a small rocky islet where you can access and lie down with your towel.

There are several ways to reach Gallipoli: by car, by train or by plane. Gallipoli does not have an airport, the closest one is in Brindisi, a town just over 50 miles away, and of course Bari, the largest city in Puglia. In any case, if your trip to Puglia starts with Gallipoli as you first stop, try to set aside a few extra days, rent a car to visit some beautiful, must-see places not too far from Gallipoli. One of them is located on the opposite side of Gallipoli and less than 1 hour by car, overlooking the Adriatic Sea. **Otranto**, a lovely town full of history, with its impressive castle, Baroque style buildings and a long, beautiful terrace, perfect for strolling, with a stunning view of the sea and the coastline. Just a few miles north of Otranto, an absolute must, is the beach of Torre dell' Orso. The beach is nothing short of amazing to see, with beautiful rock formations of the white coast, a natural arch, crystal clear sea, sandy beach, rocks on the water to jump from, simply amazing.

Continuing north towards Brindisi or Bari, another place along the way worth a stop or even an overnight stop, is the town of **Lecce**. This town is not on the coast, but it is not too far away. Same type of architecture as Otranto, but much larger in size, this city has lots of history, beautiful squares, art and museums. **Ostuni** is another small but very charming town. Sitting on top of a hill, Ostuni offers the opportunity to take the best photo even before entering it. Approaching the town from afar, you can't help but stop and photograph its ancient white houses that stand out against the surrounding landscape, so beautiful.

A very famous town near Ostuni is Alberobello with its striking trulli. (I described Alberobello and the trulli on page 50). Then **Monopoli** e **Polignano a Mare**, two coastal towns with gorgeous beaches and their picturesque old towns with lovely alleys so pleasant to stroll through. The town of Polignano a Mare is perched on a cliff above the clear waters below, an incredible, suggestive sight to watch from different angles of the town itself, giving you the opportunity to take many evocative photos, perfect for framing.

Where to sleep in this region? I suggest a masseria, a kind of farm where once lived the peasants. Built with their typical stones and bricks, these buildings in some cases were owned by families of noble origins and even had walls surrounding the property. Today these farms have been renovated in order to offer their guests the comforts of a modern accommodation without sacrificing the true experience of being in touch with nature. There are several to choose from in this southern part of Puglia.

A little further north is the seaside town of Termoli, in Molise region, with its ancient fortifications and the 13th century Svevo Castle. Stroll through its pretty medieval hamlet and you will find Rejecelle, the narrowest alleyway in Europe (walk sideways!). An hour by ferry from Termoli, you can reach the Tremiti Islands, a micro-archipelago, made up of pristine waters, beautiful beaches, a charming village, and spectacular views. Not to be missed.

All for fun and fun for all resort areas: so far, in this Seaside Places chapter, I have described the top 3 luxury resort areas (plus 1) and many other places that are distinguished by the uniqueness and beauty of the natural territory, as well as the beauty of the cities and towns built in those areas. People have different desires and ideas for their vacations. I will mention a couple of places that are not known for the scenic beauty of their territory, but for the wide range of services they offer to tourists visiting those places, and for those who seek from their vacation entertainment rather than untouched nature.

The location that has reigned supreme as the queen of fun in Italy for decades is the seaside city of **Rimini,** in the Emilia Romagna region, on the Adriatic coast. It is said that New York is the city that never sleeps, I have always said that Rimini is the city that never rests... in summertime!

If you are looking for a place where you can find many choices that keep you entertained at all hours of the day and night, Rimini is definitely for you! Miles and miles of beaches, endless choices of hotels for all budgets, shops open till 2:00 or 3:00 am, restaurants, clubs, waterparks like the Aquafan in the town of Riccione (my favorite in my early 20s), among all the rides and events it can keep you entertained for days... here you will find it all here!

Rimini is the party capital of Italy and attracts crowds of young people, but at the same time it can be the perfect place for families with children because of the variety of things to do that many hotels offer their younger guests, so they are busy having fun all day while their parents nearby can just relax.

In addition, most hotels offer full, or half board packages, which include breakfast and a 2 or 1 full course meal, making it easier (only a few steps from the beach to the hotel restaurant) and more convenient that going out to eat. Hotels are generally run by family members who add that touch of family hospitality that is more enjoyable than going to a franchise hotel.

Another theme park in the area is "Italia in Miniatura" Italy in Miniature. This Park showcases most of Italy's extraordinary beauties in one place. In one day, you can travel all over Italy, islands included! I particularly enjoyed "visiting" Venice, beautiful and fascinating even though it is reproduced to scale.

Obviously, "being" in Venice I took the opportunity to do something Venice is most famous for: taking a gondola ride, and it was fun. Italia in Miniatura is a great idea on how to spend a day in Rimini, a fun way to learn a little bit of Italian geography, admire all the most important monuments and landmarks Italy is known for and where you can find them, all while taking great pictures and...feeling like a mini giant for a day. www.italiainminiatura.com

Finally, another place you absolutely should not miss while you are in Rimini is **San Marino**, The Most Serene Republic of San Marino to be precise.
Just a 10-mile drive from Rimini and you will be abroad! San Marino, a microstate strategically positioned on top of a mountain at about 2500 feet above sea level, with a population of just over 30,000 inhabitants, is the 5th smallest country in the world, one of the oldest, with the oldest republic.
It is said to have been founded in 301 AD. San Marino is truly a charming place to visit, its position on top of the small mountain, Mount Titano, which can be reached by car or by cable car, makes this small country even more suggestive. Perched on the highest point of the mountain stands the beautiful, imposing, visually striking castle. You can get there by following a pleasant and scenic path to the top of the mountain. With its large surrounding walls, the ancient, historic the castle (a must-visit) overlooking the city and the entire valley from every angle, it is the perfect location for picture perfect...well yes, pictures.
Strolling through the small alleys of San Marino, stopping in the cute shops (also with good deals for the different tax rate) enjoying a typical meal from the surrounding area, make a visit to this microstate very pleasant.
By the way, don't forget to bring your passport with you to enter the country.

Viareggio and **Forte dei Marmi**. These two locations just on the opposite side of Rimini, are the Tuscan version of Rimini, but slightly more upscale.
Among other things, what I like most about these two towns is their geographic position, they are practically halfway between two cities to the south, Lucca and Pisa, known worldwide for their historic buildings and monuments, and the two areas of **Cinque Terre** with the nearby village of Porto Venere to the north, so famous for their wonderful landscapes and picturesque villages. (Pisa and Lucca are described in the chapter on Tuscany.) Cinque Terre and Porto Venere are beautiful in several respects. Cinque Terre (Five Lands) located in the southern part of the Liguria region, are a collection of five villages along five miles of rocky coastlines between two promontories. The five villages are all so picturesque, the old pastel-colored houses overlooking the sea, the tiny inlets, small beaches and bays, as if out of a beautiful painting of a typical Italian coast hills, greenery, cliffs, colorful villages overlooking beautiful turquoise waters. Picture perfect or painting perfect I should say. The five villages, **Riomaggiore, Manarola, Corniglia,**

Vernazza and **Monterosso** can be reached by local train or by sea. I suggest choosing this option and perhaps returning by train, seeing the villages and jagged coast from a boat is an opportunity not to be missed. The villages connect to each other via a long trail, which includes (reopens in 2023) the famous Via dell'Amore, Way of Love, that is the (lovely) name of the 1 km long, narrow, very scenic coastal pathway, a favorite of the hiking...lovers out there.
Porto Venere. Simply a gem. This enchanting village located on the southern peninsula of Liguria, just south of Cinque Terre, has it all. Breathtaking views, pastel-colored buildings lined up next to each other, beautiful small peddles beaches and crystal-clear water, an islet in front of the village easily reachable with a 5-minute boat ride, and a medieval fortress atop the cliff overlooking the village. I loved every minute spent in Porto Venere.
Taking pictures of the village, the bay and the fortress on top of the tiny, uninhabited island (just a beach, a restaurant and a couple of B&Bs) is simply an incredible sight. Forte dei Marmi and Viareggio being so close to both areas, make it a convenient starting point for day trips to all these nearby locations, while staying in a well-served seaside area with amenities and things to do.
In Viareggio and Forte dei Marmi from the beach you can admire the imposing chain of the Apennines in the background, with your feet in the sea. Look at the huge mountains as you wallow with the fish around you. Quite a feeling.

Campsites in Italy: going to a campsite can be a very good choice. For many reasons. First, although campsites in Italy are mostly located near seaside resorts, there are also many throughout Italy near lakes, mountainous areas and near cities. Because of this, it is the best choice for some. It combines the best of both worlds. You are in the city or in a popular and busy beach area, but at the same time entering a campsite you have your own oasis of tranquility in contact with nature.
It is a bit like taking a vacation within a vacation. Often at campgrounds you can find amenities not available in many hotels; swimming pools, bicycles to ride around the campsite, or doing other sports, entertainment, live music and more. Other services are available at campsites, such as free shuttle service to the nearest bus or train stop to go to the city center, mini markets just for its guests, and on-site restaurants and pizzerias. When I was in my 20s, I worked for a summer at the front desk of a campsite just outside downtown Rome. I have nice memories of both the international atmosphere of the campsite and, the good food and pizzas. They offer several accommodations, you can bring your own tent, camper or RV, rent a bunkbed, bungalow with or without a kitchen, cook under the stars, go to their on-site restaurant, or do a little of both. Indeed, campsites are a good option loved by many. www.camping.it

MOUNTAINS AND LAKES

I just mentioned the Apennines. In most cases, the first things that come to a tourist's mind when thinking of Italy, are its beautiful cities full of history, monuments, arts and culture, or beach resort destinations such as the island of Capri, Cinque Terre and so on. Aside from its incredibly rich historical and cultural heritage and despite being surrounded by water for most of its territory, Italy also has as an incredible landscape heritage to offer its visitors when it comes to mountains and lakes.

Mountains

If your ideal vacation is one of complete relax in a lonely mountain cabin while admiring the sunset with snow-capped peaks in the distance, taking walks in a quiet mountain village, if you love climbing or hiking on solitary paths, or if skiing is your passion, but at the same time you want to enjoy the comfort, the luxuries of a ritzy mountain town, or take your children to a well-equipped national park, Italy has it all.

With two major mountain ranges in its own country, the Alps running west to east on the northern border, and the Apennines from north to south for nearly 1000 miles, (which is why the Apennines are called the backbone of Italy) such a vast territory forms its own flora, fauna, habitat, offering many options to choose from, for travelers who want to see and experience something different every time they venture into a new mountainous area and region.

Suffice it to say that the summit of Europe highest mountain, Monte Bianco (White Mountain, or Mont Blanc as the French call it) at an altitude of 4800 meters (almost 16000 feet) is in Italy's smallest region, **Valle d'Aosta**, (Aosta Valley). This region, which borders with France and Switzerland, is a wonderful example of breathtaking mountain landscapes and lakes, year-round ski resorts, and is home to Italy's oldest national park, Parco Nazionale del Gran Paradiso, which, as one English writer said, is truly a Paradise of beauty. The park is very well organized, with guided walks, hiking paths, mountain huts can also be rented there.

Driving through the valleys of this small region is a pleasure and a discovery at the same time, with its fast-changing sceneries of bright green valleys and towering mountains, frozen lakes and striking waterfalls, (the most beautiful and visited being the waterfall of Lillaz in the Cogne area) secluded hiking trails, abundant wildlife, hearty food, castles, so many castles and fortresses can be found in Valle d'Aosta. Despite being such a small region by surface and population, it has over 120 castles, making it the most fortified region in all Europe. Castello di Saint Pierre and Forte di Bard are certainly among the most impressive castles in terms of size and position.

There are several villages in Valle d'Aosta and my favorite is Courmayeur. I was 14 when I went there with my parents for the first time, it was August, the hottest month of the year, and I hiked with a guide. I still remember the long walk-through small paths, overcoming the 1000 feet uphill by crossing paths. It was a bit challenging at times not wearing the proper (to say the least) shoes. Why did I do that difficult mountain trek wearing clogs? On a day trip to the pretty town of Courmayeur, we were strolling wearing light jackets, shorts and clogs, when I saw a sign for a scenic tour starting 5 minutes later. We had no other clothes or shoes with us, and when you are 14 you think you can handle anything. An impromptu moment for sure but I managed, and after about 1 ½ hours of hiking we arrived at our destination.

The sight opening before our eyes repaid us for all the efforts to reach it: we were in front of a small glacier surrounded by imposing mountains with white peaks, a frozen lake of an incredible crystal blue color, the peaks reflecting on the lake, and small icebergs floating on the water. Purely amazing.

From Courmayeur you can reach France in about 30 minutes, passing through a tunnel about 10 miles long that connects the two countries. In most parts of the Valle d'Aosta, the signs are in Italian and French indicating the proximity to that country. I have always liked seeing dual languages signs in border towns, I felt they gave a more international feel on both sides.

The Alps on the Italian side extend from Valle d'Aosta to Piemonte and Lombardia regions. On the northeastern side of Italy in the regions of Trentino-Alto Adige, Veneto and Friuli- Venezia Giulia, the mountain range of the Alps is commonly known as the Dolomiti. There is a reason for this name, which is what differentiates this side of the Alps from the northwestern ones and makes them unique. So much so that in 2009 the Dolomiti were awarded a Unesco site. The rocks are composed mainly of the mineral dolomia and because of this geological feature, unique in the world, every day when the peaks of the Dolomites are hit by the light of dawn and dusk, they turn in a warm orange color.

A truly spectacular, awe-inspiring sight: orange-reddish peaks, the immense landscape of the surrounding valleys is something unforgettable. During the long winter, when the bright orange of the peaks contrasts with the white of the snow all around, or in summertime, when the beautiful shades of green of the pine trees and the grass all over the mountain pastures, it is always the right time to visit the Dolomiti Alps. Just like on the western side of the Alps,

also on the eastern side, mountain lovers can enjoy a wide range of activities, from hiking, to trekking, to skiing and snowboarding, to cite just a few.
If your idea of a mountain vacation is to be pampered with all the comforts and luxuries that a city can offer in a mountain setting, **Cortina d'Ampezzo** is the place for you. They call it the Regina delle Dolomiti (Queen of the Dolomites) and once you are there, you will understand why Cortina has earned such a grand title, but in the meantime, I will give you some clues.

Nestled along the Ampezzo Valley, surrounded by peaks of breathtaking beauty including 6 peaks over 9000 feet high, spectacular mountain passes, waterfalls, a glacial lake of stunning beauty, lago di Misurina, from where you have an incredible view of the stunning Three Peaks of Lavaredo.
The lake is at an altitude of almost 6000 feet, with a small beach for sunbathing during the summer, just 10 miles from Cortina, absolutely a must see if you are in that town. There are also some beautiful lakeside hotels if you want to spend the night in a quieter setting, just between you and nature. With so much variety of things to see and do, Cortina makes it a perfect fit for everyone's desires.
This glamourous town is known to be visited by celebrities who like to spend their holidays in the mountain in a ritzy setting with 5-stars hotels, luxury boutiques, upscale gourmet restaurants, and exclusive clubs. It is also loved by families with children thanks to the numerous family-friendly activities available. A visit to the Helmut Ulltich Astronomical Observatory to admire the vault of heaven and the starry sky of the Dolomites, or the Paleontological Museum, would certainly be a fun, interesting, and educational experience for everyone.
For outdoor activities it is possible to rent mountain bikes, go ice skating or take long walks admiring the local nature with easy paths suitable even for small children. Otherwise for a massive fun packed day your children will be grateful to you for years to come, you can take them to the famous adventure park Cortina Adrenalin Center, where they can walk on Tibetan bridges, jump over nets, cross in suspension and much more. www.adrenalincenter.it

What if you are not a rich celebrity or you do not have children, but still want to have fun doing sports that will pump up your adrenaline? Here are a few options for you: Nordic skiing, ski mountaineering, kite skiing, snowboarding, curling, snow shoeing, dog sledding (yes, that too), and even fat tire biking (if the tire hits a nail becomes fat and flat tire. That's not flat-tering. I propose to name it wide tire or grand tire. By the way, do you know why a bike can't stand on its own? Because it's two tired).

If you are a climbing enthusiast, Cortina it's up your alley with a variety of rock-climbing locations near and far where you can practice this sport at different levels. Excursions and guided tours are also available, and information can be obtained at the tourist point office in downtown Cortina or at the hotel where you are staying.

Cortina has a reputation for being an exclusive destination, and of course hotels play an important role. A wonderful example of this is the Cristallo Luxury Collection Resort and SPA. This iconic 5-star resort situated in an amazing natural setting, exudes opulence and tradition, grandeur and elegance, attention to details in every corner, and unparalleled services, providing an unforgettable stay to its guests.

How to reach Cortina from Venice (about 100 miles): of course, you can rent a car, otherwise from Venice airport and Venezia-Mestre train station, the Cortina Express Bus is a comfortable and economical way to reach Cortina. www.cortinaexpress.it Other alternatives are taxis or a car rental service with chauffeur. If you prefer to save time, enjoy incredible views and make an entrance with glamour in the glamourous town of Cortina, the helicopter service is the perfect option for you. www.airservicecenter.it

Cortina d'Ampezzo, can be visited and enjoyed all year round. The Queen of the Dolomites truly lives up to its name. With its majestic peaks, fairytale landscapes, lavish resorts, and luxurious services, this top-notch destination will inspire you, pamper you, and make you feel a bit royal too.

If you would like to visit the Dolomites and have a touch of both Italian and South Tyrol's feel, you might want to head to the Trentino-Alto Adige region. This region is located east of Veneto and the two main cities, Bolzano and Merano are bilingual as are other smaller towns in the area. As in Valle d'Aosta where signs are written in Italian and French, in Alto Adige all signs are in Italian and German.

With a population of over 100,000 inhabitants, **Bolzano** is the largest city in this part of the region. It lies on a large flat valley surrounded by mountains. It is an interesting city that encompasses two very different cultures, Italian and Germanic, beautifully blended on the same ground. Bolzano and its entire province are part of Italy for a little over 100 years, since 1919, after Austria lost part of its territory during the First World War. You can admire historical buildings and monuments from both cultures, Gothic and Romanesque architecture can be seen in many churches, monuments and arcades around the city.

Piazza Walther, the main square of the old district of Bolzano, is a beautiful and historic square with a cathedral, fountains, a garden full of flowers,

colorful buildings all around, restaurants and café' with their distinct typical Italian or Austrian pastries or dishes to choose from. A really nice atmosphere to breathe, so to speak. I am writing about Piazza Walther and just turned to look at a framed photo hanging on the wall at home. A beautiful morning in Piazza Walther on a sunny day in August 2016.
Most cities have museum of various kinds: history, art, science, etc. In Bolzano there is a museum where you can see something truly unusual dated about 5000 years ago in incredibly well-preserved conditions. Otzi the iceman. It was found at the end of the 1990s in a glacier. If you go to Bolzano meeting Otzi is a must! www.iceman.it

From Bolzano you can see the peaks of the Dolomites from afar, but it doesn't take long to get to the mountains, or a national park, and Bolzano is a great and well-connected starting point to many popular ski destinations in different directions. I remember we took a train and in about 1 hour we arrived in **Merano** or Meran, as they say in German. This old town just north of Bolzano, has a more distinctive Tyrolean flavor due to its buildings and streets being closer to Austria. The old buildings have a more austere look softened by the houses with the colorful geranium flowerpots in the windows typical of the Tyrol.
Merano is a renowned spa town, which is why thousands of people flock to this mountain resort every year. It offers wellness programs with thermal baths in a well-equipped, state-of-the-art facility, surrounded by beautiful mountain views. You can take long walks in a mountainous setting, relax sitting on a bench listening to the pouring waters of the Merano river, and stroll through the pleasant town. If you are looking for wellness and tranquility in your mountain holiday, Merano is for you. www.termemerano.it

Of course, skiing, sledding and hiking in the beautiful settings of the South Tyrolean Dolomites, indulging with the typical earthy Tyrolean and Italian dishes, are also great reasons for a vacation in Merano or the nearby mountain towns of Vipiteno and Bressanone.
As I mentioned at the beginning of this chapter, Italy has two major mountain ranges, the Alps from north-west to the north-east side, and the Apennines, from north to south. Due to their geographical position and conformation, the Alps are very famous for their high peaks, glaciers, boundless valleys and breathtaking landscapes. Pretty towns have sprung up in these areas, which have become famous mountain ski resorts.
The Apennines are a different type of mountains in a geographical sense, with much lower peaks and milder climate than the Alps. Nevertheless, even in the

Apennines range there are several ski locations, especially in Abruzzo region. In **Roccaraso** there are ski slopes of over 50 miles with varying levels of difficulty. Being from central Italy, I went to many ski resorts in the area. I will tell you about a couple of them that stood out more than others.

Mount Terminillo, less than 70 miles east of Rome, also called the Mountain of Rome because of its proximity to the capital, is the perfect choice for thousands of Romans to spend the weekend skiing without travelling too far. The resort area is called **Pian de Valli** situated at an elevation of 5300 feet.
Growing up, with my family I went there many times for a day trip or a week-long stay. I still remember the names of the beautiful hotels on the main (and only) square, the cozy restaurants with local cuisines, and the café' where I would go in the afternoon to enjoy a cup of hot chocolate after spending the day snowboarding or going up the mountain (with the ski lift) to learn how to ski. There was a movie theater, small shops and even a disco!
The movie theater is no longer there; you can find a mini market and few other shops instead. If you have children and thinking of going to Terminillo during the summer, an adventure park is waiting for them, the Squirrel Park, where like the one in Cortina, they can have fun on suspended bridges, trails and much more. www.terminilloexperience.it Pian de Valli is not a typical village, but a resort destination for a pleasant holiday to the Mountain of Rome.

At the foot of the mountain, (only 15 miles from Pian de Valli) is the old town of Rieti, nice to walk along the cobblestone pedestrian street with its many small shops. I was there in 2021 and enjoyed listening to the "roaring" sound of the Velino river and taking long walks on the sidewalk near the riverbank. Speaking of roaring, a mighty roaring sound is the one that comes from the Marmore Falls, the highest waterfall in Italy. A spectacular scene to admire. It's located just 15 miles north of Rieti, so again, if you are in the area, take some time to visit the park and the waterfall. Keep in mind that the falls are closed for a few hours during the day. Some of the powerful water from the falls is used to generate electricity for the entire surrounding area.
For some info www.cascatadellemarmore.it. the site is in Italian only, (click on "orari e aperture" and then "rilascio acqua", which shows the water release time and the visiting hours. The schedule, made up of numbers, should be understandable). If you want to do some high-intensity sports and don't mind getting a little wet, there is a canoe and rafting center in the area.

Pescasseroli, (altitude 3800 feet), is a picturesque village that rises in a wide plain right in the heart of the Parco Nazionale d'Abruzzo, (the National Park of

Abruzzo). Incredible views of unspoiled nature and a mountainous landscape all around. Among other animals, the park is home to deer, roe deer, chamois, eagles and sometimes it is possible to spot a brown bear from afar. The park is quite large, you can visit it by car for a longer tour, by mountain bike or on foot, choosing different routes to follow or take a guided tour. It is best to start the visit to the park by first going to the Park Visitor Center located downtown, which will give you a good general idea of the park. www.parcoabruzzo.it

Pescasseroli is a multifaceted destination that attracts visitors all year round. In winter it's a prime ski resort area. Many ski slopes to choose from, including the bold black diamond for the more experienced. Others, however, do not go there for sports, but to do something different, take the cable car up to the top of the mountain to admire the scenery and nature all around, spending the day playing in the snow with the family.
This location is a paradise for those who love hiking or horseback riding, in the area there are riding stables that offer special programs for children. A charming old village with a small historic center with narrow alleys full of colorful flowers, noble buildings, artisan shops selling goods typical of the area in a setting with activities for a pleasant family-friendly mountain getaway.

Lakes
When one thinks of vacations, escaping the hustle and bustle of a chaotic city or just leaving a hectic routine behind, most of the times the mind r to a seaside resort. Many times, however, and especially at the peak of the summer season, the beaches can be quite crowded. I have never thought of a lake as a second choice over the sea, but as a different option to choose from for a vacation or a day trip.
Lakes are quite fascinating, going to a lake is like being immersed in a timeless tranquility. The blue color of the lake, the green of the grass and trees around it give a feeling of relaxation. In addition to the greenery of the surrounding nature, the charm of the villages that overlook the lake is also a rather nice setting. In my personal top 10 of favorite cities and towns to visit in Italy, one of them is on a lake. Which one and where? I'll tell you when we get there.

Another good thing about the lakes are its calm waters that make it easier to practice some water sports like paddling a canoe or a boat. When I go to the lake, at times I gaze upon creatures so beautiful at sight, the swans. They are so graceful and elegant in all their essence and unaware of this. The lake's water always so calms it is their element, the lake looks more beautiful with the swans. Such a serene sight, they truly complement each other.

Indeed, lakes are truly a fascinating thing. Have you suddenly yearned for a lake tour? I do! There are so many lovely lakes and gorgeous locations in Italy it will be quite difficult to choose just one as your favorite. I'm going to describe the most remarkable lakes for their beauty and peculiarity and list them from north to south. All the lakes in the north are alpine and those in central Italy are of volcanic origin.

Lake Orta, in Piemonte region. Given its relative proximity to other large lakes such as Maggiore, Iseo, Garda and Como, it is often overlooked especially by international tourism. The residents of the area do not mind that, as they can keep the lake as a hidden jewel to themselves. And this small lake it really is like a jewel, with a center stone that makes it even more unique and precious. What is the center stone? The islet lying precisely in the center of the lake, the island of San Giulio, full of trees, small houses towered by a Basilica with frescoes of the 15th century. Ah, when nature, culture and art blend so harmoniously together like they were made for each other! The island can be reached by a small ferry taken from the port of the characteristic village of Orta San Giulio.

Lake Maggiore. As the word says, Maggiore (Major, but you've probably figured it out) is really a major lake, in fact is the 2nd largest lake in Italy, located on the south side of the Alps. It is also very long: its western shore is in Piedmont, its eastern shore is in Lombardy, and its northern tip is in Switzerland, on the Italian-speaking side, Canton Ticino. The lake, stretching for such a long distance, has several small towns along the shore on both sides, with Arona, Stresa and Verbania among the main ones.
As I mentioned earlier, most of the times villages bordering lakes surrounded by the greenery of the natural environment form a beautiful whole, and these towns are not exception. It gets even better as you get closer to these small towns; you start to see more details. People strolling along the lakefront full of small shops, café and restaurants, and through the narrow streets of the quaint old downtown with historic buildings. Yes, most towns look alike, but then again, each one has its own peculiarity and here the peculiarities are outstanding. Stresa lies in an amazing position: facing the lake and the enchanting Borromeo's islands, if this picturesque sight is already so beautiful, it is even more so when looking into the distance, with the mountains framing the lake. The quaint town of Arona is larger than Stresa, it is very pleasant to walk through the alleys full of shops and eateries, the lakefront with the view of a castle on the other side of the lake, and the mountains in the distance. Going on a cable car amplifies the amazing sights a thousand-fold: looking at

the view from above allows you to catch more details, especially of the Borromeo islands which are simply magnificent.

The Borromeo islands are a set of 3 very small islands, Isola Madre, Isola dei Pescatori and Isola Bella. Since the 12th century they have been owned by the aristocratic Borromeo family. The heirs of this important dynasty are still the owners of the small islands, which attracts countless tourists every year. www.isoleborromee.it The islands have a population of just a few dozen people plus those who go to the islands to work in souvenir shops, restaurants and a couple of hotels (a hotel on a miniature island on a lake surrounded by mountains, a rather unique setting to find!).

Isola Bella (Beautiful Island) is the closest island to the mainland and the most suggestive. Palazzo Borromeo was a residence, now a monument, of truly extraordinary beauty. It is hard to believe that 450 years ago this same place that we can admire, the superb residence with the Baroque Garden, trees, houses and everything else in it, was just a huge rock surfacing on the waters of the lake. This Baroque Palace has marvelous interiors, richly decorated royal hall, salon of Honors, masterpieces by artists such as Raffaello and Correggio, ten tiers of exquisite terraced Italian gardens, fountains and statues, even a beautiful grotto to remind us of marine environments.

Their special guests, the splendid peacocks that roam the gardens, enhance the beauty of the area, their elegant feathers and the small "crown" on their heads are a perfect match for this princely location. In relation to the royal subject, Emperor Napoleon and his wife lived in this Palace for a while. Even Queen Victoria in the 18th century did not miss the opportunity to spend some time on Lake Maggiore, visiting all the amenities on the lake and the islands during her holidays all the way from England, a very long journey with much less comfortable means of transport than those we are accustomed to today!

Isola dei Pescatori (Island of Fishermen) neighbors to Isola Bella and is a very pretty thing to see when approaching it by boat, the cluster of houses, trees and restaurants lining the edge of the lake offering a truly scenic view. This island is the only one out of the three that is inhabited all year round and has about 60 permanent residents.

Isola Madre is the largest of the three islands and what is outstanding is that it is one of the oldest botanical gardens in Italy. This very extensive garden with rare trees such as the Kashmir Cypress or the Gingko Biloba, exotic and colorful flowers such as the rhododendrons, makes it a very fascinating place to wander around. In addition to the luxurious garden, another great touristic attraction on Isola Madre is the Palace Borromeo, built in 1590 with rooms and halls beautifully decorated, is another great reason to visit this enchanting island. Between Spring and Fall, a trip to Lake Maggiore and its miniature islands is absolutely worth the time, adding it to the list of destinations in Northern Italy. An interesting mountain-lake route in the area is the Vigezzina Railway, which connects the characteristic mountain town of Domodossola (reachable from Stresa or Verbania) to Locarno, in Switzerland. 52 km of dramatic mountainous terrain and landscapes, 83 bridges and 31 tunnels to cross, with stops in places like Santa Maria Maggiore, a charming tiny village. www.vigezzinacentovalli.com The famous chimney sweep festival is held in this village on the first weekend of September, attracting visitors and chimney sweeps from all over the world (there is also a chimney sweep museum).

Lake Como. Lago di Como, in Lombardia region, at the foothill of the Alps, it is the deepest lake in Italy (1350 feet) and the most famous Italian lake known internationally. Since Roman times, the lake has been a popular holiday retreat. Although it is fascinating to look at all year round, especially in the warmer months the colors of the lake, the greenery around contrasting with the towering mountains, makes the lake even more attractive.

During the sun-kissed summer, the sweet pleasures of the breeze on the skin and to the eyes for its stunning views, the picturesque towns and villages overlooking the lake, the historic and luxurious villas with their beautiful hanging gardens full of colorful flowers, the piers for boat rides, all contributes to the charm that surrounds Lake Como. Wealthy entrepreneurs, celebrities, cross the ocean to spend relaxing moments in their villas on Lake Como.

The lake has many towns along its shores. The most important is, of course, the one that gives the lake its name, Como. A very pretty and ancient town on the southeast end of the lake, Como was founded by the Romans in 196 B.C. on the site of a Celtic village. The old district is very pleasant to stroll around with many artistic sites to visit, precious monuments and beautiful views.

The most outstanding monument is Duomo di Como which features a very interesting appearance. The reason is simple: it was erected to replace the Romanesque cathedral of Santa Maria, built in 1015, so it presents added architectonical styles such as the Gothic façade, while the sides are of Renaissance time, but still looks very harmonious. Palazzo Broletto built in 1215 is attached to the Duomo. Bonardo da Cadazzo, the mayor who commissioned the project did so wanting to show the interrelationship between the two authorities, religious and political, over the diocesan territory. Villa Olmo is another Como landmark. This monumental 18th century villa with its impressing fountain right in front of the lake with its vast, elegant park is certainly wort a visit. Then, after visiting Villa Olmo and its park, if you are in for a splash in the water's lake, very close to Villa Olmo is the Lido Villa

Olmo, a well-equipped beach club where you can rent sunbeds and umbrellas, laze in the beautiful garden, grab a bite at its café' or swim in the pool.
From Como you could also take a historic cable car that connects Como to Brunate, the lake to the mountain I would say. Inaugurated in 1894, the cable car ride takes only 7 minutes to reach the village of Brunate and sitting on this historic train is quite an experience. The ride is very steep with over 1500 feet of elevation gain in 5 minutes, to be on it is quite an exciting experience indeed! The hill climb allows you to see breathtaking views of the city of Como, the lake and the mountains all around. A must do. It is noteworthy to mention an important inventor who was born in Como. With his bright (literally!) idea he improved the quality of people's life from then to the present day. Alessandro Volta from Como invented the electric battery in 1799.

Lecco is the 2nd most important town on the lake. In an impressive mountainous landscape setting, at the end of the southeastern side of Lake Como, Lecco is probably the city with the most beautiful view of the lake. Just like Como, also Lecco was "born" as a Celtic village before the Romans took over. The downtown pedestrian area is nice to stroll around, the shops, café' and restaurants with their outdoor tables from where, while enjoying a nice dinner or a tasty gelato, you can admire the view of the massive mountain rock and the lake right at the end of the street.
When thinking of Lake Como, the mind immediately goes to a location, chances are you are thinking about it too...right now! Bellagio, called the Pearl of Lake Como, is an exquisite tourist resort. Its charming location, on the tip of the promontory that divides the lake into the two branches of Como and Lecco giving the way to a very suggestive landscape, this quaint village with its colorful houses, picturesque alleys and stairways, beautiful gardens and luxurious villas from the 18th century, Bellagio is certainly a Pearl among the treasures of Lake Como.

Lake Garda. The largest lake in Italy, it shares its waters and 100 miles of coastline with Lombardia, Veneto and Trentino Alto Adige regions. All three lakes, Maggiore, Como and Garda have an elongated shape, although Garda differs at its southern end. In fact, Garda Lake has a very different shape and landscape from one end to the other, the northern end is long with a narrower tip and is surrounded by mountains, while the southern end is very broad, ringed on a valley that extends all the way to the Po valley reaching Emilia Romagna region. Just like the other lakes, and being even larger, lago di Garda has a lot to offer in terms of striking mountains sceneries, charming towns to visit, and beautiful beaches. Let's start touring the main towns and villages of this massive lake. I must say that the word massive, even if I appropriately referred to Garda Lake because of its enormous size, applies equally well and even better when referring to the Alps and Dolomites Mountain ranges. They are massive by definition! They are incredibly wide and tall rocks that stretch for hundreds of miles, towering everything around them with their presence, and this lake is no exception.

On the northernmost side of the lake in Trentino region, lies the town of Riva del Garda. This lovely town overlooking the lake is also surrounded by imposing mountains. The glance of the overall view is simply astonishing. Although further away from all the other Garda's towns, Riva del Garda is so beautiful that it is no wonder that year after year it has become one of the favorite holiday resorts in the entire area.

Lots of greenery, olive and lemon trees, plants and flowers on the lakefront with panoramic views, ancient historic district with its brightly colored houses, arches and narrow streets, a medieval bell tower that stands tall in the center of the town's main square, Piazza III Novembre, a beautiful square surrounded by porticoes with a view of the lake. There is also a small castle, which houses an interesting Civic Museum with the remains of the ancient lake village.

Riva, as the locals call it, is very pleasant to visit. It also has much to offer as entertainment especially during the summer. An event that has become a famous tradition in Riva del Garda is called Notte di Fiaba (Fairytale night). Every year, at the end of August, the town organizes four days of theatrical performances, games, workshops, concerts and fairytales stories such as Robin Hood or the 4 Musketeers, all performed near the picturesque setting of the lake. A fun, family-friend event that attracts many visitors of all ages. www.nottedifiaba.it (the site is in Italian, but you can get an idea).

Riva del Garda is also the perfect spot for lovers of sport. Thanks to the wind that blows almost every day on this side of the lake, there are perfect conditions for any water sport, from wind surfing, paragliding, kite surfing, cycling along the shore and even rock climbing on the lake, all of which are very popular in this area. You can find several beautiful beaches with breathtaking views of the nearby mountains on both sides, from the Sabbioni Beach all the way to Torbole Beach, some with grass and some with small peddles, all stunning and perfect for a sport or relaxing day at the lake.

I mentioned that in Riva del Garda you can see lemon trees, going a little further south of Riva on the western side of it, in Lombardy, there is a charming little village that is all about lemons, so much so it has Lemon in its name: that is, Limone sul Garda. Centuries ago, Limone was the place known for growing lemons. Rich in lemon groves making the air and the gastronomy of this small town unique. Limone sul Garda it is not only lemons, but also a quaint resort village with narrow cobbled streets, ancient buildings, beaches, and paths for pleasant walks along the lake.

Jumping across the lake on the Veneto side, a very pretty and elegant village is Malcesine. Very picturesque view from afar and even better, from the lake during a boat ride, from where you can admire the blue waters of the lake, the old town on the shore, the magnificent Scaligero Castle that towers over it and the impressive mountains behind. A jaw dropping and picture-perfect view. The castle houses a museum with historical curiosities. A cable car ride up to the nearby Monte Baldo offers the opportunity to enjoy an incredible panoramic view of the lake, the town and, of course, the ancient castle.

By the way, if you are a bride who dreams of getting married in a princely castle like in fairytales, I am probably doing you a favor by letting you know your dream could come true. The top wedding venue in the entire area is Castello Scaligero. Then two of your dreams will come true at the same time: Your Dream (Wedding and) Vacation To Italy!

Going further down we find another pretty village, Lazise, wrapped in ancient walls and with a well-preserved Scaligero castle. Lazise is known for its thermal baths, very calm waters, not only children love to swim there, but also swans are often seen floating on the placid waters of this side of Garda Lake. Lazise, being a quaint and relaxed resort location, makes it very suitable for families with children and anyone who wants landscapes, tranquility and relaxation from their vacation.

On the southern tip of Lago di Garda lies the town of Peschiera del Garda, located between two ancient fortifications, is rich in historical interests. Centrally located at the end of the river Mincio where it merges with Lake Garda in a position that in ancient times would have been considered very strategic, on three very small islands and the two fortifications built to protect the town.

Today, these islands and their short bridges add to Peschiera's charm. There is in place an efficient transportation system connecting Peschiera with larger cities like Verona, Brescia, Mantova and Milano, about an hour away.

Peschiera attracts hundreds of thousands of visitors every year, thanks to the beauty of the lake and beaches, its old town with historic buildings and bridges, as a starting point to another exquisite nearby town, Sirmione, and finally, to its proximity to the largest and most famous amusement in Italy and one of the most renowned in Europe, Gardaland. This park resembles the typical theme park you can find in the US or elsewhere, with a different flavor.

I call it all-in-one theme park, because, unlike other places where each park has its own theme, Gardaland has several, but all in the same location. Convenient. For a fun packed day with rides, shows, events, good food and much more, Gardaland is the place to go. www.gardaland.it

A few miles west of Peschiera del Garda, there it is: Sirmione! Stunning, jaw dropping, spectacular Sirmione. Situated on a peninsula only 2.5 miles long and at its narrowest point 400 feet wide, Sirmione showcases a gigantic artistic and historical heritage in the smallest territory. The only access to Sirmione is through the small drawbridge in the central portico and the first thing that awaits you is the monumental Rocca Scaligera Castle. This fortress built in the 13th century is surrounded by the beautiful waters of the lake, adding beauty to the area of the castle. It included two crenellated towers, mighty walls, a dock used as protection against invaders and a collection of Roman sculptures.

So evocative, just looking at it captures you back to Medieval times. (You may wonder why there are so many castles in the area with the same name, Scaligeri. Well, Scala was the name of a powerful dynasty in Veneto during the 12th century, and Scaligeri was how they were referred by).
Next to the castle is where the ancient village offers another glimpse into past times. Simply walk through its historic center, with arcades, small and narrow cobblestone streets, each offering incredible views of the lake.

Restaurants, shops, souvenirs to buy local products are everywhere, as well as everywhere you look around there is the charm of this ancient village. Going toward the tip of this tiny peninsula you will see Le Grotte di Catullo, some Roman ruins of what a Roman villa was built in the 1st century AD.
An incredible place to build a villa, with unparalleled 360 degrees views. Just below there are also pretty beaches and a park with benches and beautiful trees, perfect to get some shade and breeze during the hot summer. Sirmione is an amazing place to visit at least once in a lifetime. By the way, this is also one of my favorite top 10 places to visit in Italy.
Lake Orta, Maggiore, Como and Garda are all served by an efficient navigation service, with comfortable ferries and hydrofoils connecting all lake towns to each other. Some also offer daytime sightseeing cruises or evening dinner cruises on board, or dinner cruises at lakeside restaurants.

Lake of Braises. Since this alpine lake is located in the heart of the Dolomites, I was a bit undecided whether to include Lake Braies in the mountain portion (as I did for Lake Misurina near Cortina), but this lake is so extraordinary, it's worth a trip on its own like the other lakes I just described. Lago di Braies, also called "the Pearl of the Dolomites", is the most famous lake in the Alps. Although the lake is in a secluded area, visitors from all over the world come to admire this Pearl that is also a UNESCO World Heritage Site. The lake is in Trentino- Alto Adige region, in the South Tyrol area of the Dolomites at an altitude of nearly 5000 feet (1500 mt). The imposing mountains around the lake with their snow-capped peaks and the green conifers near the shore are mirrored in the lake, giving it an amazing sight. The varying shades of green in the lake's pristine waters, and its crystalline transparency offer an overall scenery of a disarming beauty.

The wooden stilt house on the lake (from where canoes can be rented) adds a characteristic touch that blends in with the surrounding environment. Looking at the southern shore of the lake you can see the imposing mountain whose peak reaches over 9200 feet, the clouds at that height are often near the top of the mountain increase its charm for more striking pictures. By the lake there are pretty beaches, picnic areas and trails for nice walks around the lake. Lake Braies (also called Pragser Wildsee in German) is about 1 hour north from Cortina (about 30 miles) on a not very wide but scenic mountain road, with views of high peaks, green valleys and small villages that recall the typical Swiss or Austrian pastures. Summer is high season and especially from mid-July to the end of August it can be very difficult to find parking (there are not many spots anyway). I recommend arriving early in the morning and booking your parking spot online and in advance. These are two official sites, www.lagodibraies.com and www.pragsparking.com

Lake Trasimeno. This lake in Umbria region, is the fourth largest lake in Italy. The lake is circular, the main town is Castiglione del Lago, a pretty little town with a mighty castle. There are three small islands in it, Polvese, Isola Maggiore and Isola Minore. To be really accurate, Polvese and Maggiore are not so small after all, considering that Isola Maggiore is more than 1 mile long of which most are fields full of lush trees, a cute old village where about 15 inhabitants live, and others who go to the island to work in the few small restaurants and café'. There is also a landmark on the island, Villa Guglielmi, a building between an ancient villa and a castle overlooking the lake.

Polvese Island is even larger than Maggiore, all its territory is a natural park mostly used as an olive grove. Furthermore, on this island there is a huge castle, Castello Isola Polvese. Even if there is no village, it is still open to visitors for overnight(s) stay at the Fattoria (Farm, but do not worry, no animal to take care of or work of any kind!) where you can enjoy earthly meals and do some sports including learning archery, or, for a more upscale experience there is also a small resort with a beautiful garden to relax in. In Lazio, the region where I was born and spent most of my life, there are several lakes. Bolsena the largest, lake Vico, lake Albano which has a pretty beach and the cute small village of Castel Gandolfo, nearby Nemi lake, and other smaller lakes. The most famous however, is lake Bracciano.

Lake Bracciano. I am particularly fond of this lake, because of its proximity to Rome I have been there countless of times over the years, from when I was a little girl until I moved to America years ago. For a day on the lake beach, a pizza on its shore, or simply for a walk with friends through the cobbled alleys of the pretty town of Anguillara, (one of the small towns on the lake) it has always been very nice to go to lago di Bracciano. The swans that floated on the lake were also so beautiful to watch. I once saw a black swan and, between surprise and amazement, I remember thinking "wow, there are not only white sheep and black sheep, also white swans and black swans!". The white swans looked elegant and graceful, the black swans fascinating and mysterious, I could not decide which one I liked more. Ok, after this walk down memory lane, let us continue from where I momentarily left off. Lago di Bracciano, being only 40 minutes north of Rome, is a quick escape from all the hustle and bustle of the city, a change of scenery in the outskirts of Rome. Although not as famous and glamourous as Como, this lake has been a favorite location for celebrity weddings, set of movies, and TV series like "Everybody loves Raymond", the episodes of their Italian vacation were filmed in Anguillara.

There are three pretty towns built on the shore of the lake, the largest, from which the lake takes its name, is Bracciano. This ancient town is mainly known for its imposing castle, il Castello Orsini Odescalchi, a medieval castle built in the 12th century. It is worth taking a tour inside the castle, from the top floor you can take great pictures of the old town below, the castle and, of course, the lake. Anguillara Sabazia, is another charming town built on a promontory with great views of the lake, the town and the pier. Anguillara is perched on a hill and the narrow cobblestone streets, the small houses attached to each other as in a cluster, give the feeling of being in an ancient village.
Trevignano Romano is the third town on the north side of the lake. It has a nice piazza on the lake front and a boardwalk with a small beach right in front of its downtown. The medieval village quarter is a nice area for strolling, and the Archeological Museum has an interesting collection of Etruscan objects. There are many cafes and restaurants in all three towns where you can sit, enjoy beautiful views and a local meal in a relaxing and not overly crowded environment. Yes, lakes are an excellent choice for a beautiful vacation!

BEST WAYS TO TRAVEL THE COUNTRY AND GET THE MOST OUT OF IT

I have travelled all over Italy all my life by every means of transport, car, train, bus and of course, by plane. From my years of experience, I have concluded that travelling by train is by far the easiest and most comfortable way to travel in this beautiful country (unless you must be from Milan to Palermo in less than 2 hours, then the obvious choice is the plane). Several reasons led me to this conclusion, so let's explore all the options.

Trains. First and foremost, Italy is well connected by a network of high-speed trains, intercity trains and regional trains that cover the entire territory. This is of course, the most important factor in choosing whether to travel by train, if the railroad system is not well connected (and on time), there is no point in choosing the train.
That said, when travelling by car you can easily find yourself sitting in traffic, both that of a big city or that of the highway, especially from mid-July to the end of August when pretty much half of the Italians pour into the highways as that is the period when most of them go on vacation. When you travel by train on the other hand, the only place you will be sitting is the comfortable seat of a carriage that will get you to your destination on time, observing ever-changing scenery along the way, relaxing by reading the newspaper and a snack that will be provided (on selected trains and fares). If you are hungry, you can simply get up and go to the dining car, enjoy a meal with a view, and when you arrive, get off at the city center, where everything is close at hand.

Let's go into a little more detail about the type of trains. High-speed trains are modern, super-fast trains, easily reaching up to 360 km (225 miles) of speed in minutes connecting large cities in no time. For example, it takes less than 3 hours to reach Rome from Milan (almost 400 miles away) on a Frecciarossa train. This type of train only stops in major cities. Whether your departure or arrival point is not in a big city, the other option is the intercity train, which stops in both large and smaller cities. Finally, the regional train stops at all stations, from large cities to very small villages. Because of the frequent stops, this local train is the least fast (however convenient and punctual).
There are two major railway companies to travel across the country. Trenitalia www.trenitalia.it is the primary one, it is owned by the Italian government and has a very widespread network of stations throughout Italy. Italo www.italo.it is a privately owned railway company; it operates only at high-speed connecting many of the major cities. Prices: depend on the type of train

chosen and how far in advance the ticket is purchased. Sometimes, with both Italo and Trenitalia, you can find nice deals on their website, but only if tickets are purchased well in advance and seats are still available at the lowest fare. Trenitalia's high-speed train Le Frecce (The Arrows) and the Intercity sometimes offer discounts for families or for travels in certain days of the week. In addition, on Trenitalia's overnight long-distance trains, you can choose your seat, berth or a sleeping cabin with private bathroom and shower, and the next morning, a hot breakfast served in the cabin making the trip more comfortable.

Speaking of trains and comfort, if you love trains and unique experiences, where train travel is as memorable as the places you want to visit, where while traveling you will indulge to an unforgettable experience and excellence, this happens when the words train, dream vacation, and luxury are tied in a three-word name that stands as symbol for all of this: The Orient Express. This train of such iconic name, with a vintage yet sophisticated décor that exudes class and elegance in every detail, offers packages of carefully selected 2 or 3-day itineraries in different cities and regions of Italy. On board you will be transported (literally and in its essence) on a dream vacation of another era, savoring La Dolce Vita on The Orient Express. www.orient-express.com

Going back to the train purely as a mean of transportation, there are times when travelling by train is not the most suitable option. As widespread as the Italian railway system is, in many rural areas there are no railways, and while these areas are mostly reached by bus it can take a long time to do so. Or, if it is not a rural area you are going to, but you are planning to take a long tour through the countryside, taking your time and stopping whenever and wherever you like, renting a car may be the best option. Let's talk about cars.

Cars. Driving a car obviously has its good pros. Ability to drive in less touristy areas, choose which route to take, create your own itinerary, escape the beaten paths and choose back roads, stop when your eyes catch something special and live a more authentic experience. While doing all this you roll down the car windows, feel the summer breeze on your skin and enjoy that wonderful feeling of freedom (if you do not travel during the summer forget the summer breeze and keep the car windows up, you can still enjoy the wonderful feeling of freedom though). Furthermore, you don't need to use public transportation.
Along with the pros there are also some caution and cons: in Italy almost all cars have a stick shift (I read a couple of years ago that the ratio was 90%

manual and 10% automatic) if you don't feel comfortable driving a manual shift, I suggest you to book your car rental well in advance requesting a car with automatic transmission, it could be more expensive, but you will find it.

Throughout Europe gas is 3 to 4 times more expensive than in the US. Consider this if you are budget minded, and the highway has tolls (to give you an idea, as of today the Rome-Florence route is about 20 euro). Finally, the most annoying con of renting a car is driving it in large cities with their usual traffic and congested roads. Difficult, at times nearly impossible to park, you can find yourself wandering around the area ending up leaving (unless is the month of August, remember? The month when half the Italians pour into the highways, which is also my favorite time of the year to drive in Rome, enjoying the half-empty city and finally finding a parking space easily, hooray!)

One more thing you need to be aware of, is a sign with these 3 letters: ZTL, Zona Traffico Limitato, (Limited Traffic Zone). Most of the historic centers of any Italian city have ZTL set up to reduce traffic and pollution in these areas, allowing only residents and delivery workers with a pass to go through. The fine is very expensive and all you have to do to get it is ignoring the ZTL sign by entering the ZTL zone, the camera on top of the sign will do the rest to make sure you will receive the hefty fine delivered to your door (even if you live abroad). The ZTL sign also shows the time when it is active, most of the time from 8 am to 8 pm, but some last longer. Most historical landmarks are in the central area of any big city, which is the same area bounded by the ZTL and where public transport converges. Local trains, buses, cable cars and subways are all interconnected, making it easy to go around and enjoy the sights without thinking about traffic, ZTL, search and pay for parking.
Tickets for buses, subways and cable cars can be purchased at any newspaper stand. In Rome, a single ticket cost 1.50 euro and is valid for 100 min from stamping, (cannot mix bus and subway). Daily ticket is 7 euro and offers 24 hours of unlimited rides on any bus, cable car and metro. It is 12.5 euro for 48h, 18 euro for 72h, and 24 euro for a week. Children under 10 years old travel free with an adult. Other cities might have similar offers.

Ferries. Italy, with over 5000 miles of coastline, 2 major islands, many small islands and archipelagos, makes boats, ferries and hydrofoils indispensable. One of the nicest necessities however, the purchase of the ticket comes with incredible views and a breeze even in the hottest summers. I always enjoy going on a ferry. Nice to sit on the top floor, photographing the view that opens before our eyes as we pull away from the coast, seeing the landscape with details that we could not enjoy if we were not on a boat or a ferry. Going to Sicily, the view from the ferry as it departs from the mainland in Calabria already seeing the Sicilian coastline, its jagged landscape, the lights of the cities, is truly fascinating from both sides. From Naples the view from the sea towards Sorrento, or Capri, Ischia and Procida, is so beautiful. I recently took a ferry from Naples to Procida, what an amazing view along the way, I took a photo of a lighthouse standing on a very high promontory in the bay of Naples, stunning! From La Spezia to Portovenere, you can see the bay, the colorful houses, the fortress at the top, all so unforgettable. I never think of the ferry as just a means of transport, but as part of the fun of a vacation!

There are many ferry and hydrofoil companies in Italy that operate in every direction. Long distance ferries, such as the Genoa-Palermo or the Civitavecchia-Olbia to name a couple, are very large ferries with restaurant, bar and swimming pool. Depending on your budget, you can book a comfortable armchair or a private cabin. This website www.directferries.it lists all the main options on each route. For long distance routes, the suggestion is to book well in advance, while for short routes (Naples – Sorrento) you can also buy the ticket directly on the dock before departure. By the way, if you are in Naples and you are thinking of going to Sorrento (you should, so charming and in a fantastic location), I recommend going from Naples by ferry or hydrofoil, and return to Naples by the local train, the Circumvesuviana, so you can admire the landscape from both perspective, sea and land. (In the morning, the train is more crowded, better to catch it on the way back to Naples). If you plan to visit the excavations of Pompeii or Herculaneum, this very inexpensive trai stops in both places. (Napoli – Sorrento route) www.sorrentoreview.com for schedules.

Planes. With some 40 airports, Italy is also well connected in terms of flights. The Italian flagship carrier is the new ATI taking the place of Alitalia, which succumbed mainly to competition from low-cost airlines, very numerous in Europe. For this reason, very low fares are often found even for last minute flights, both domestic and throughout Europe. Just like American budget airlines or those from other countries, low fares refer to the seat only, then add carry-on luggage or suitcase if you have them. Flying within Italy is a great idea if you are traveling long distances, have limited time, and if flying is much cheaper than the train (which, sometimes is the case).
The high-speed train from Rome to Milan takes less than 3 hours from the center of Rome to the center of Milan. The flight Rome – Milan takes 1 hour, you need to be at the airport (which is usually far from the city center) well in advance to check-in, going through security it can become time consuming, many prefer to

travel by train. Considering the addition of luggage, the transfer costs to and from the airport, for the budget minded even a cheaper flight deal on a mid-haul distance, could prove to be more expensive than expected. If you want to search for a flight deal, not all websites show low-cost airlines, but these two do. www.kiwi.com and www.kayak.com

Buses. Yes, the bus can be another alternative for traveling in Italy. Buses manage to get to those places where trains do not go as some rural areas in the Dolomites or in southern Italy. Also, if booked well ahead, they can be dirt cheap. Sure, it can take longer to arrive, but buses can be a good option if you don't have time constrains. Furthermore, modern buses have comfortable seats, air conditioning and free wi-fi. In large cities, buses leave from the airport or the square in front of the main train stations, while in small towns where there is no train station, they usually leave from the main town square. A new fleet I like is www.itabus.it modern, very comfortable and ecofriendly. If you are also planning to go abroad, www.Flixbus.it can be a good option.

Cruises. ok, this is not exactly traveling within Italy, it is more traveling around Italy. Having the shape of a long boot surrounded by the sea over almost the entire territory, two major islands and many smaller ones, many ports from north to south, it can be visited by traveling from the sea. Therefore, a cruise with Italy as an itinerary, may be a good option, one that has its conveniences. You do not have to pack and unpack, or go to the airport, train station or long hours on the highway to go to other places. Most of the time, the ship doesn't stay too long in one place to fully embrace it, but it allows you to get an overall idea of it while you can always enjoy amazing views from the sea to the coast.

If you choose a cruise, I would like to give you two noteworthy suggestions: try to take extra days before or after the cruise, (if the cruise starts and ends in two different cities it's even better, you could take a few days before and after the cruise visiting different areas) so you can also spend more time ashore, see other attractions at your own pace and try local foods.
My other advice is to choose an Italian cruise line, so you can enjoy the Italian atmosphere on the ship. MSC CRUISES is a Neapolitan cruise line of excellent quality, with beautiful itineraries around the peninsula and the Mediterranean to choose from and state-of-the-art facilities. Among the many comforts, services, entertainments this cruise line offers to its guests, also delicious gourmet dishes and the famous Neapolitan pizza, giving you the opportunity to try authentic Italian cuisine even on board a ship. www.msccruises.com

ITALY ON A BUDGET

First of all, let me preface one thing: having a budget does not in any way mean that you can't have fun or experience a vacation you have been dreaming of, that you've long imagined. Having a budget simply means... being more creative! I find the word "creative" to be a really good word, it exudes positivity, doesn't it? Being creative means just that: creating! Finding different ways to turn an idea, a project, into reality.
The more we care about that project, the more we will find ways to make it happen. So, keep dreaming and start creating!

If you have a budget in mind, the first thing to do is to grab a pen and paper and outline the things you would like to see and do on your trip. Gathering as much information as possible and planning is the key to a successful trip (this applies to all trips, not just the ones with a set budget). After deciding what you would like to do and see, you have to "work" with that budget, and this is where you start to get creative.

You could start getting creative by choosing the time of year to travel. At certain times of the year, traveling costs more. In Italy, July and August, as well as mid-December through January 6 and Easter week, are high season. Flights are also more expensive during these times, so if circumstances allow, it is best to choose other dates. Not only are airfares to go to Italy more expensive, so is traveling within Italy and more challenging to find good deals. However, by booking well in advance you may be able to find some discounted prices if you want to travel during those months.
At times, the same can happen for very last-minute departures; sometimes to fill the last available seats, airlines are willing to offer very discounted fares. If you do not have work constraints that prevent you from grabbing the offer and leaving on-the-fly (literally), this can be a good option.
In the previous chapter, I included several links where you can find different carriers and the discounts they offer. If you are planning a beach trip to Italy, instead of July and August another good option is May, June and September. Much cheaper and less crowded.

Where to stay and eat. Hotels near monuments, in historical areas or by the beach, are notoriously expensive. Also, you want to consider which cities you plan to visit. In a very large city like Rome, it is not too difficult to find centrally located hotels that are fairly affordable. If you are going to Venice, finding an affordable hotel can be challenging and sometimes nearly impossible, but just outside of Venezia, in Mestre, or even in beautiful Padova, you can find reasonable rates. A cheaper and a smarter option is to rent an apartment. Airbnb is a popular website for home rentals, but sometimes the additional fees can make it a bit too expensive. Other sites offer broader deals. This site, www.trivago.com brings together the various options from all the other sites, whether you want to book a hotel, a B&B, to rent a room or an entire apartment, so you can compare and choose everything in one place.

Renting an apartment comes with the "freebie" of feeling like a local. There is no front desk reception at the entrance, you come and go as if you live there. Not only do you feel like a local, but you can act like one and save significantly. The apartments always have a kitchen, so why not take advantage of it? Go to a nearby supermarket, take the time to browse the shelves, the fridge counter, or the wine selection (much cheaper than in the US). At the bread counter you can choose from the many types of excellent Italian bread, freshly baked pizza, cold cuts and cheese, also in the frozen food section you can find gourmet dishes made with simple ingredients and ready to eat, so you do not even have to cook, just warm up and enjoy it.

If you have more time, you can also go to the local fresh markets, they are in every town and village all over the country (especially on Saturdays), for some seasonal fruits and vegetables at a bargain price.

When I visit a foreign country, going to a local supermarket is part of the travel experience and I always take the time to go there, I am curious to see what products they have and what is different from the country I live in. I always want to try foods from the place I am visiting, and at times, I bring something back to America (I always bring a few boxes of my favorite cookies from Italy!). As I said, going to a supermarket is part of immersing yourself in the local culture, and often saving a lot too.

If you want to eat out as well, I totally understand, after all you have come all the way to Italy, so you should absolutely do that....picnics are a great idea! Bring with you what you bought at the supermarket and a tablecloth from the house you are renting, lay it all out on a lawn in a park with a beautiful view of the city, or the lake, or the beach, and ecco qua, (here you go) you're in Italy....eating out!

Jokes aside, (although it is a cute idea and I do love picnics) when you are on vacation, you want to taste the local dishes of the place you are visiting, not just the ones from the supermarket. Especially when visiting Italy, food is such an important part of the vacation, so we cannot miss it, can we?

There are several ways to spend little money and enjoy something typical during your holiday in Italy: street food is one of them. No matter where you are in Italy, you will find places where you can buy a panino, a stuffed pizza or some other finger food while you walk around, they are cheap, good, local, and satiating. I will talk more about Italian street food in the next chapter.

Vacation is also going to restaurants, sitting outside enjoying the outdoors and the view of our surroundings while tasting a good meal. At lunch. This is the budget chapter and lunch is cheaper!
Many restaurants display the sign with the set menu, you can choose from 3 or 4 options, spending between 10 to 15 euro and have a nice Italian lunch. Not a gourmet meal, a traditional dish from the area. Not only do the touristy restaurants near the main landmarks offer the fixed menu, but there are also many small family – run restaurants here and there that do so. (Keep in mind that most of the time the bread on the table is not free even if you don't ask for it. Yes, in most restaurants bread it's a given, but they don't give it away!) So, as you walk, when you see a restaurant you like, look at the menu and keep it in mind, most likely there are others nearby, take another look and compare, choose the one that inspires you the most and... buon appetito!

With over 500 museums, archeological sites and monuments that can be visited throughout its territory, Italy has an artistic, historical and cultural heritage of inestimable value. Culture has its own importance and one of the reasons Italy is known all over the world is for its historical monuments. Many of them I have briefly described in the pages of this book. Visiting museums and archeological sites is part of the experience of visiting a country. It is where we learn, marvel and become culturally enriched.

This culture that enriches us has a small cost, the entrance ticket. Sometimes, for reasons of budget or limited time during our vacation we do not go to museums. The good news is that many museums in Italy are free on certain days of the month. As of today, in Rome, on the first Sunday of the month, most museums and archeological sites are free (for the Vatican Museum it is the last Sunday of the month, and you must get in by 12:30 pm). Also, the wonderful Royal Palace of Caserta has free admission on the first Sunday of the month.
When museums have free admissions lines are always especially long, so keep that in mind if you are short on time. On the other hand, because some museums are free every day, there is not a huge turnout of the public on just a set day, making admission faster. If there is a particular museum or site you'd

like to visit, you might want to check online to see if /when it's free. In any case, for some museums like the Uffizi in Florence, I highly recommend booking online if you want to be sure you can get in and visit.
Often in cities and towns, many monuments are usually located in the same area not a great distance from each other. This is a great thing because it makes it easier to find them, and although local transport in Italy is quite cheap, walking is the cheapest means of transportation, it is free. Walking is also a free gym: it helps you stay in shape after all the new food samples. Not only is the famous "a walk in the park" an easy and good thing, but so is a walk in the city!

In addition to "free" transportation (for kids under 10 it really is) and free museums, there are other things that are free and fun to spend pleasant evenings organized by cities, such as summer events. In the pages where I wrote about Rome, I mentioned the summer at the Tiber Island and at Castel Sant'angelo, and the summer of Fairy Tale Nights at Riva del Garda. Events like these are held in many places and are definitely budget friendly, allowing you to enjoy yourself without having to open your wallet, unless you decide to give in to some sweet or savory temptation to taste!

So many things affect the budget of a vacation. I have mentioned the most important ones, but there are other factors that contribute to planning a great vacation. Personal preferences for example. What is very important to some is not important to others. With the same budget, some may be particularly thrifty and stretch every dollar in order to stay more days and see more places, while others prefer to use their budget by indulging in perks and comforts but staying fewer days.
Speaking of comforts, as I have already said, a stay in a campsite can be a good option especially if you like being in the middle of nature and with ample space to wander around relaxing after a day at the beach or sightseeing. In a campsite, you can choose a simpler and spartan stay by bringing your own camping tent or a more comfortable solution by renting one of the bungalows available on site. In addition, campsites are equipped with many amenities for a comfortable stay, there are swimming pools, mini markets, restaurants and entertainments for their guests, for a pleasant stay without breaking the bank.

One thing is for sure: admiring breathtaking views of cities, sea, bays, lakes, mountains, landscapes, is priceless! For everything else there is a credit card, but the breathtaking views are one of the few things that are free (of charge).

FOOD (and my favorite places to eat when I am in Rome)

Sure, the historic cities, the monuments, the art, the culture, the breathtaking views, the Tuscan hills, the Italian coast, the islands, the sea, the mountains, the lakes, the fashion made in Italy, are all excellent reasons to visit Italy, and even just one of them is worth the trip. But there is one thing that Italy is so famous for, loved, celebrated, imitated. The same thing talked about in magazines, broadcast on countless tv shows, taught in classrooms, and that makes us happy....ok the title of this chapter gives it away. Yes, you guessed it, I am talking about food, cibo.

Food in Italy is an institution, culture, a topic of conversation. I myself, whenever I call my parents in Italy, during the chat I invariably ask, "what did you eat today?" We are so passionate about food that not only we talk about it, but we can also have serious conversations about it. Good food is a serious matter, delicious food is a very serious matter. Seriously...good!

Food is also history. I am sure you've had a Margherita pizza, have you ever wondered where that name comes from? Well, that pizza was created in honor of Queen Margherita of Savoy visiting Naples in 1889 on the occasion of the unification of Italy. The pizza maker thought of making it with the colors of the Italian flag, the red of the tomato, the white of the mozzarella, the green of the basil, and named it after Queen Margherita. Who would have thought that behind a simple and delicious pizza there was a piece of history! For the pizza maker, food was a seriously good matter, and no matter where we live, now almost 150 years later, people all over the world are still enjoying his famous pizza Margherita, the queen of pizzas.

For some, a vacation to Italy, is all about sights to see and meals are just that, meals, the local cuisine is not one of the reasons for their trip. For others it is the food and wine experience that brings them here, they want to be totally immersed in the food culture, take cooking classes (which are fun) and bring home the new skills they have learned. Most want to combine both.

In Italy cuisine is not only seasonal, but also regional. Each region has its own specialties that you cannot find in other regions. I love that each region has its own individuality, the local dishes are made with typical ingredients of the area, when traveling it is nice to notice the different dishes and ingredients on the menu, without the cookie cutter style.

I was recently in Umbria, the region where truffles grow. I love truffles and of course when I went to a restaurant on the lake I looked to see if they were on the menu. Homemade ravioli stuffed with black truffles: simply fabulous!

However, if you are visiting Rome (to name a city) and you would also like to taste Sardinian or Sicilian cuisine, you can find a Sardinian or Sicilian restaurant in Rome that offers in its menu only specialties of their territory.
So, which are the typical regional dishes? There are so many, because every region has its own local dishes, its desserts and many of them its own wines too. It would take a long time to list all the specialties region by region, and city by city. Yes, there are also specialties typical only of that city. Last year I went to Viterbo, a quaint and characteristic ancient town less than 2 hours north of Rome. While walking around, I noticed that most of the restaurants had the same local specialty on the menu, a dish made with chestnut cream. Being that I really like chestnuts, this caught my curiosity and attention, having never seen this dish anywhere else before going to this town.

Climate also influences the type of food we eat. In northern Italy, especially in the mountains, in the **Alp**s and **Dolomites** area, the climate is very harsh in winter, the dishes are very rich and energetic. Lots of earthy flavored food. Potatoes, polenta, meat, foods that give the energy to face a day outdoors. If you are planning a mountain vacation, you will find many dishes made on these ingredients. Polenta is made from corn, but a little different from the type used in America. The corn used for polenta is the coarser type.
There are many polenta-based dishes, and they are delicious. Polenta with meat on top, often sausage or ribs, or polenta with vegetables, with different types of sauces, fried polenta cut into squares, and the list goes on. But also, in the Dolomites you can find delicate dishes with seasonal products from their land. The blueberry risotto is one example. A combination that is certainly different from the usual, delicate and delicious. And even in this case there are many variations, only with blueberry, or blueberry and speck, blueberry and gorgonzola cheese, blueberry and chives, to name a few.
Speaking of rice, in all the regions of northern Italy above the Po ' river, the rice that has been cultivated for centuries in those areas in the paddy fields of the Po Valley, is part of the traditional cuisine of the place, the famous risotto! I love risotto and cook it often (even today for lunch actually). **Piemonte** is not only famous for its wines and where the very rare and precious white truffle grows, but also for its rice dishes made with these local specialties. Risotto al Barolo, with its distinctive flavor of Barolo wine, and the finest white truffle risotto, are staples of that region for those who have refined tastes.

Speaking of staples and rice, in **Lombardia**, risotto Milanese with saffron is so well known and loved by the locals it has become the most traditional and famous dish of Milan. The aroma of saffron in the air is so pleasant and even more so the taste of its distinctive flavor, simply delicious. Both risottos have a bold flavor, and if like me, you love truffles or saffron and you are in those regions, it is a must to try these two recipes. Another typical Milanese dish is cotoletta alla Milanese. This cutlet is actually a simple recipe, but it is the type of meat, preparation and cooking that make the difference. Another typical dish of Milan is ossobuco alla milanese, a very old dish, whose recipe dates back to 1700. Really delicious, with a good sauce on top in which to dip the bread. I must say, even if it is not the Milanese recipe, the best ossobuco in the world is the one my mother makes, ciao mamma!

Milan is famous in the world for its panettone. Yes, panettone was born in Milan. This soft traditional dessert can only be found between October and January, so if you are in Milan or Italy during that time, treat yourself to a slice of panettone, much better if freshly made from a local artisan bakery.

Do you like pesto? I do, and where does the pesto recipe come from? Well, the label on the jar you buy at the store clearly says it, pesto Genovese. Of course, the pesto in the jar is a far cry from the fresh pesto, even the fresh pesto is not quite the same as the fresh pesto in **Liguria**. It is the basil grown on that soil, the exact combination of ingredients, the way it is prepared, the best pasta with pesto I've ever tasted was in Liguria. If you travel to that region, trying their pesto pasta is a must. Another local dish is sciattamaiu, as they call it in their dialect, in Italian "schiatta mariti" (drop dead husbands), but do not worry, there is nothing sinister lurking in the recipe for this simple, earthy vegetarian dish from the peasant tradition. In ancient times, when workers returned home, they ate so much of it they dropped...not dead, but with indigestion! A famous food to go is their thick and very soft focaccia, so good. Not for nothing, in the rest of Italy that type of soft focaccia is called focaccia or pizza Genovese. Hey, they absolutely deserve the credit for it.

The **Emilia Romagna** region has an incredible food tradition. Just think that fettuccine, ravioli, tortellini, cappelletti filled pasta (or stuffed pasta as they say in America) come from there. The quality, the flavor of this fresh egg filled pasta is so good, full-bodied, that it doesn't need anything else. The traditional recipe for tortellini con carne and cappelletti is to cook them in broth (homemade broth of course). That's it. So simple, so delicious. Just add some parmesan, or parmigiano Reggiano as the locals say, by the way, the very versatile parmigiano cheese is another delicious product of this region.

While we are on the subject of pasta and condiments, I'm sure you've tried the famous lasagna alla Bolognese, with red ragu' and bechamel sauce. Mouthwatering. Go to Bologna and try them again, deliciousness on another level. The famous Prosciutto di Parma comes from Parma, a city in Emilia Romagna. What about mortadella, or Bologna as they call it in America? You know that one. I mentioned just a few traditional dishes, all of which are famous worldwide, that show the incredible richness of the gastronomic culture, love, and passion people of this region have for food. The special relation they have starts from the selection of ingredients to the final result, a pleasure for the palate with that pleasant overall feeling of getting up from your chair at the end of the meal, a sense of satisfaction after enjoying not only a meal, but a beautiful moment in life.

I just wrote about pleasure for the palate. Interestingly, a restaurant that for many years has been voted as the best Italian restaurant to date, is located in Emilia Romagna, in the city of Modena. The very exclusive three-star Micheline restaurant Osteria Francescana, will take you on a journey, experiencing food at a new sophisticated level, with refined ingredients and highly aesthetic presentation of the courses. www.osteriafrancescana.it Reservations must be made well (months) in advance.

On the other hand, sometimes even a quick food to go can also be good, satisfying and typical of the area. In the coastal area of Emilia Romagna, in Rimini and other nearby towns, you can find their local staple, crescione. It resembles a calzone, but is lighter, and you can choose from many different flavors. My favorite is always potatoes and mozzarella, so yummy!

Toscana is very famous for its wines; the good soil of the Chianti area has been generous for centuries with its farmers who work hard in order to bring its excellent wines to the tables all over the world. Of course, Tuscany is not just wine, the Florentine steak is certainly the most famous dish of the region. This high-quality steak comes from bred in the southern part of Tuscany. The cows, which can weigh over a ton, follow the same routine today they did 2500 years ago, spending the day grazing on grass in the fresh air of the hilly Chianina farming area.

It's not just about meat in Tuscany, there are famous traditional dishes that are vegetarian and vegan. Fagioli all'uccelletto, made with cannellini beans, the ribollita a must-try with kale, or pappa al pomodoro made with 2–3-day old bread. They all have few ingredients and spices in the recipes, and in their simplicity these humble earthy dishes are so full of flavor. When less is more. Schiacciata. There are 2 types of schiacciata in Tuscany, the Florentine sweet schiacciata , a dessert cake that is only available from January to March during Carnival time, and the more famous savory schiacciata, a type of focaccia resembling a flat bread. It tastes even better sliced in half and filled with cold cuts, which, brings me to a place right in the heart of Firenze, where you can taste the schiacciata filled with all sorts of cold cuts, grilled veggies, cheeses, and other condiments to choose from. The long line at the entrance of this shop testifies the incredible success of this eatery. The name? All'Antico Vinaio, via dei Neri 76, Firenze, just a two-minute walk from Palazzo Vecchio, a must try when in Florence. I mentioned Chianti wines and the schiacciata dessert, another small sweet typical of this region are the cantucci, a hard and sweet biscuit with almonds, perfect to dip in Vin Santo, a sweet Tuscan dessert wine, they go so well together!

Let's go more south, to another region rich in culinary tradition, humble with simple ingredients and bold with flavor. A region that is the emblem of a dish that everybody loves, from a 3-year-old child to 125 years old great-great-great-grandma-and-pa. I am sure you have guessed what I'm referring to, but if you need another clue, here it is: if I say Napoli what is the first thing that comes to mind next to the word "food"? Yes, pizza napoletana! This is the region of **Campania**, the birthplace of pizza. The place where a piece of dough with few simple basic toppings, cheese and tomato sauce, got us all hooked and even changed the way we think about the days of the week. Have you ever heard people say "tomorrow is our pizza night" referring to it as a that-day-of-the-week-habit for a pizza dinner? It did change the way we think about the days of the week! Pizza is certainly what defines Napoli when it comes to food, and one of the reasons why tens of millions of people visit Naples and Italy every year, to enjoy an authentic Italian pizza.

Neapolitans take pride in their beloved signature dish, they are master at it, difficult to find a place where they don't make good pizza. Granted, some places top others and are renowned among the locals for both the fragrance and the toppings used. Although I prefer Roman pizza, which is thinner and crispier, I also really like Neapolitan pizza, I always have one every time I go to Naples, enjoying it with the flavors of the local toppings used there. What if you are gluten intolerant, but would like to try a traditional Neapolitan pizza? No worries, a restaurant in Naples makes all the dishes on their menu also gluten-free. www.mamaeat.com There are also 3 locations in Rome and 1 in Milan. Campania, with so much coastline, also has a long tradition of seafood. Spaghetti with clams, cooked and flavored to perfection. Although risotto is a northern tradition, risotto alla pescatora (risotto with seafood) is one of the staples of this region, as is pasta with potatoes and pasta with zucchini.

Everywhere in Naples you can find a great selection of street food. Fried pasta, cuoppo, (a paper cone, the cuoppo, holding deep fried food like small potato croquettes and panzerotti, or fish, small meat nuggets, tempura vegetables, stuffed dough pockets), pizza with scarola (sautéed escarole), fried pizza, pizza al portafoglio (translates wallet pizza, it's a smaller round pizza folded in 2 or 4), cuzzetiello (the crusty end part of a loaf of bread filled with meatballs and sauce, or vegetables and cheese). Neapolitan paninis, croquettes, and more. Prices range from 2 to 7 euro. For a quick, cheap, local and satiating meal on the go, you cannot go wrong with any of these. All very good, none very light, but hey, you're on vacation.

After the street food snack or meal, it's time for a dessert or a good espresso. Gran Caffe' Gambrinus, in via Chiaia 1, next to piazza Plebiscito, is THE pastry shop par excellence. This classy, elegant and historic coffee house of the 19th century is a landmark in Naples and for all Neapolitans. Absolutely a must see. At Gran Caffe' Gambrinus you will find a great selection of delicious pastries. The two most famous internationally are the baba', a pastry filled with rum, and the sfogliatella (called lobster tail in English, it looks more like a shell though), a crispy pastry filled with cream. These two staples are so popular you can easily find them in any Neapolitan pastry shop. In addition to that, I would be doing you a disservice if I did not tell you about my favorite Neapolitan mini- pastry on the go, the delightful fiocco di neve (snowflake). Always a must when I am in town. Here is where you can find it: Pasticceria Poppella, via Santa Brigida 69/70, Napoli. Choose two or three flavors, sit back and slowly savor this literally delicious moment (with eyes closed, of course!).

From Naples, for a unique experience off the beaten tourist path, you can visit Paestum, about 70 miles from Naples. Not only is there a beautiful Greek temple to visit, but there is also a beautiful masseria, a farm nearby, where you can see the process of making buffalo mozzarella and have breakfast of local yogurt, milk and cheeses in a delightful natural setting. A beautiful day with a unique experience to remember. www.masserialupata.it

I have already briefly mentioned it in the description of Sorrento, if you go to Sorrento do not miss the chance to try their signature dishes from that small area, Gnocchi alla Sorrentina and Linguine with lemon. Both delicious!

They don't just use the lemon for pasta, also for cakes, cookies, and of course the famous limoncello, a strong yet delicate liqueur made from the huge Sorrentine lemons, is sold in many sizes making it a perfect gift to take home.

Let's take the ferry and go to **Sicilia**! This beautiful island has no shortage of authentic, traditional, genuine dishes and amazing desserts. What grows in this sunny land is used to fullest, even if it is something as small as the humble caper, the creative Sicilians prepare recipes where the pungent and distinctive flavor of the caper is enhanced to complement many local dishes. In Sicily you can find capers in pasta dishes, fish, tomato salad, the very tasty eggplant caponata typical of Palermo, just to name a few. Sicily is famous for its pistacchio from Bronte and chocolate from Modica. These two small towns attract many visitors every year just to taste their delicious and locally grown pistacchio and chocolate. Ricotta salata, a type of hard, salty ricotta, is another staple of the Sicilian regional culture. The ricotta produced in this beautiful land accompanies excellent local dishes such as the famous and delicious penne alla Norma, pasta with aubergines, tomato sauce and salted ricotta. A must try in Sicilia. Of course, ricotta salata is used in many other dishes and even on pizza as one the toppings, cut into flakes, giving pizza a more bodily, appetizing flavor. So good. A traditional recipe from Palermo is baked anelletti, a small ringed shaped (hence the name anelletti, from anello = ring) pasta. This baked pasta is rich and delicious, with so many ingredients that if you eat it for lunch, it will keep you full and satisfied for the rest of the day. The condiment is made of Sicilian ragu' (meat, tomato sauce and peas), aubergine, boiled eggs, parmigiano, salame, caciocavallo (a typical southern Italian cheese) and breadcrumbs. If it sounds good just by reading it, wait until you try it, you'll be asking for more.

Not only in Naples, but also in Sicily there is a wide variety of street food that will whet your appetite just by looking at it. Typical of Palermo pane and panelle (warm bread with fried chickpea flour, squeezed lemon and parsley). So yummy. My very favorite Sicilian street food are the arancini, big rice balls filled in many ways and flavors, from Sicilian ragu' to eggplant and fish, ham and bechamel, just to name a few, all so mouthwatering it's hard to pick just one. Easy to find them everywhere in Sicily although in some areas they taste slightly better than others. You could also go where the arancini were invented. Last time I was there I have to admit it was a bit difficult to choose between the over 30 different flavors on display, so much goodness and variety all at once! Rosticceria e Trattoria Famulari, via Battisti 143, Messina.

Sicilian desserts: the number one dessert in Sicily famous worldwide is the cannolo siciliano, of course! Cassata siciliana is a famous cake during Carnival. Granita with brioche and gelato with brioche are an irresistible combination. A must, must try! I have fond memories of granita with brioche. As a child, every year I went to Sicily with my parents and my two younger brothers, I still remember every morning I went to the bar a few steps from my grandma's house with an empty pitcher, the barista filled it with lemon granita, added freshly baked brioches (what a delicious buttery aroma!) and we would have this delicious breakfast before heading to the beach. What a beautiful way to start the day was for me, as soon as I woke up, I could not wait to go the little bar with the empty pitcher! The iced creamy granita with brioche is my 1st stop as soon as I arrive in Sicily. My other stop is at the Ritrovo Felicita restaurant located in Santo Stefano di Camastra, the small village I described on page 50. The address: Snc. Contrada Felicita' 6/7KM 169BIS, Santo Stefano di Camastra ME. The restaurant is easy to find about a 15 min drive on the only one road up from St. Stefano towards Letto Santo.

Puglia. The Apulians are people with a culinary tradition of simple wholesome ingredients, their staples being wheat, vegetables, and fish. I am sure you too know some of their local gastronomic products that are famous abroad. The Apulian focaccia, high, soft and with crunchy edges, cherry tomatoes, a sprinkle of oregano, a little bit of oil and a pinch of salt. Simple and simply delicious. The focaccia barese (Bari-style focaccia) is one of the most authentic and well-known staple dishes of this beautiful southern region.

What about their signature snack-appetizer-or-anything-in-between, the famous taralli pugliesi? This earthy finger food is so tasty in any flavor you choose. They make them in a long list of flavors: traditional, fennel, onion, potatoes, chili pepper, pizzaiola, cereals, turnip greens, and the list could go on. They can be sweet or savory, taralli are indeed a staple food to try and an appreciated gift to take home. The panzerotto is Puglia's most famous street food. Essential for an Apulian, but also for those who visit. Fried or baked dough with tomato sauce and mozzarella inside. The filling is so abundant, it will drip at the first bite. Just warned you!

I just mentioned mozzarella. Puglia is where they make my very favorite kind of mozzarella, the burrata. So delicious and mouthwatering, a must try! The most well-known Apulian dish is certainly orecchiette with turnip tops. A simple, wholesome pasta dish made with only 3 ingredients: homemade Apulian orecchiette pasta, turnip greens, and breadcrumbs previously sauteed in a pan with oil. Very simple but delicious dish that Apulian's know how to cook with great skill. Puglia, like Sicily and Campania, being coastal regions, all have a great variety of fish-based dishes appreciated by locals and visitors.

And now let's go to **Roma**. Rome, my city. The city where I grew up, lived most of my life and love, with its beauties and flaws. The largest city and the capital of Italy, the city of such ancient origins as to be lost in the mists of time, also has a very ancient culinary tradition. The De Re Coquinaria, the first collection of Roman cuisine recipes written by Marco Gavio Apicio, a well-known cook of the time, dates back to the time of Emperor Tiberius, (14/37 AD). With this millenary inheritance, there are in fact many Roman recipes handed down by tradition, staple foods of Roman culture and cuisine, and they are not only the main dishes. Two old and famous artichoke recipes very different from each other, one soft and moist, the other fried and crispy, both delicious, are served as an appetizer or side dish. Carciofo alla romana (Roman style artichoke) and carciofo alla giudia, (Jewish artichoke), one of the typical dishes of the Jewish restaurants in Rome. Let's take a look at some Roman dishes, authenticity and full-bodied ingredients, starting with the pasta. The most famous and loved pasta dishes by Romans and those visiting Rome, have few ingredients but a lot of flavors. You probably know some of these internationally renowned dishes. Pasta carbonara for example, made with pancetta, egg and pecorino romano cheese. That's it. A superlative dish. (Also, my favorite Roman pasta). Bucatini all'amatriciana, tomato sauce, guanciale (similar to, but it's not bacon) and pecorino romano. Amazing flavor. By the way, pasta amatriciana is not exactly from Rome, but from Amatrice, hence the name Amatriciana, a village far from Rome near Mount Terminillo.

Pasta cacio e pepe, with pecorino romano and pepper, and rigatoni alla gricia, with guanciale, pecorino and pepper. All pastas are made with a few simple ingredients, but all so bold with flavor. You can't say you have been to Rome if you do not try at least one!

What about the celebrated fettuccine Alfredo, so famous in America? There are also Alfredo sauces in jars sold in all American supermarkets. Can they be tasted in Italy as well, or are they one of those things that have Italian names, but aren't? Yes, of course they are Italian, and they can be enjoyed in all their rich flavor in Italy, specifically in Rome. Last year while strolling around Rome, I passed by Alfredo's restaurant which I knew, I have already tasted their exquisite fettuccine in the past, so I took the opportunity to go inside for a moment and look at the photos of the Italian and international celebrities who have dined at the famous restaurant over the decades. Chatting with the manager who is a relative of Alfredo, I learned how the famous recipe of fettuccine Alfredo came about. What a romantic story behind that recipe! I took their photo book with me to the US. Are you wondering if fettuccine Alfredo in Rome taste just like the ones in America? Try them and judge for yourself! Ristorante Alfredo alla Scrofa, via della Scrofa 104, Roma.

By the way, speaking of things with Italian names not found in Italy, many Italian-style restaurants in other countries have dishes like "chicken or veal cutlet over spaghetti" on their menu. You won't find restaurants in Italy where they put a slice of meat on top of a plate of spaghetti. It wouldn't occur to them to do that. Simply two different courses. A slice of meat, however, goes very well with a slice of bread, veggies, or potatoes. Pasta? Let's leave it alone!

Gnocchi alla romana are a famous dish of the Roman tradition. They are not the potato gnocchi we always see; they are made with semolina and are cylindrical discs. The recipe calls for a creamy sauce, and they are baked in the oven to form a nice crust. Delicious. If you love seafood and rice, risotto alla crema di scampi, risotto in a scampi cream, is another Roman famous dish, delicate, but full of flavor. A very famous meat dish with a very curious name (also very self-explanatory!) is saltimbocca alla romana. Saltimbocca literally means "jump to your mouth". This dish is so incredibly delicious and tasty, it will jump from your plate to your mouth in no time! An absolute must.

In a city as large, chaotic and busy as Rome, street food has been a pleasant necessity for the past 2000 years. Thermopoliums, open-air places where food was cooked and sold for take-out, were popular then. Today, the streed food scene is more vibrant than ever, with a wide variety of local street food to choose from. Romans have been fond of 3 staples for generations: suppli, croquettes and pizza al taglio. Suppli is a deep-fried rice ball the size of an egg stuffed with tomato and mozzarella covered with breadcrumbs. Croquettes are made with potatoes, mozzarella and parsley, also egg-shaped and breaded like suppli'. I have memories of being 5 years old asking my parents to buy it, and I still enjoy these snacks as much today as I did then. You can find them at a pizzeria al taglio, which brings me to the 3rd street food that Romans love, pizza al taglio (pizza by the cut.), which is not like the typical pizza by the slice. Here the pizza is not already cut into the same size slices. That's great.. and convenient!
At a Roman take-out pizzeria, you decide how much pizza you want, how big or small, 1 inch or the whole pan. Why is it convenient? Because it gives you the opportunity to try different flavors without having to buy 3 or 4 large slices. You decide how much of each type you want. "I don't speak Italian; how will they understand me?" you may be wondering. No problem. Don't Italians have a reputation for gesturing when they speak? Just point to the pizza you want with your finger and then show by gesturing how much of it you want. They will understand you. Guaranteed!

So many types of pizza to choose from, so many flavors, so hard to choose at times! I have tried them all, but the type I buy the most is always pizza with potatoes, typical Roman and not easily found elsewhere.
Pinsa romana is another local street food, as the name suggests, from Rome. Not exactly a pizza or a focaccia, but something in between the two. It comes from an ancient recipe, the classic and simple focaccia, with a consistency between a pizza and a focaccia, and pinsa has an oval shape, not round.

Speaking of something in between, the new entry made-in-Rome is trapizzino, born in 2008 in the Testaccio area, which has become a popular street food in Rome and has spread throughout Italy and abroad. A fusion that unites the two culinary worlds of Rome: a small portion of a typical Roman dish to be eaten sitting, inserted inside a white Roman pizza with a dose of geometry taken from the famous Roman sandwich, the tramezzino. The trapizzino is a sort of triangular-shaped white pizza pocket, stuffed with typical dishes of the Roman tradition: chicken alla cacciatora, eggplant parmigiana, meatballs with sauce, stracciatella of burrata with zucchini, Roman tripe, to name a few.

Then there is the king of Roman street food loved by generations of Romans: panino con porchetta, pork seasoned with salt, spices and herbs before being slowly roasted, sliced and placed in a fragrant Roman-style bread, the rosetta. It is so succulent that it is worth the trip to the outskirts of Rome to the small town of Ariccia, where the crispy, melt-in-your-mouth porchetta comes from and they master at it. Sometimes, you can find it in some street food eateries in Rome, and a restaurant in Testaccio has it on its menu (address below).

After having listed some of Rome's most famous traditional dishes, I will list some places where you can enjoy what I have described and much more. So, here is a small roundup of restaurants you could try:

Pastasciutta, fresh artisanal pasta made daily to eat in or to go, very good at a great price, from 6 to 8 euro. Piazzale Flaminio 10. www.pastasciuttaroma.it

La Fraschetta di Mastro Giorgio, a tavern in Testaccio where they serve, among typical roman dishes, the very flavorful porchetta. Via Alessandro Volta, 36.

Senza Fondo, it literally translates Bottomless, very fitting name for this all-you-can-eat Roman style restaurant. Opened at the end of April 2021, this eatery offers a selection of Roman dishes. In a touristy area, it is a good choice especially if you are in Rome for a very short time, here you can try several typical (smaller) dishes at once. Appetizers, pasta, meat, sides and pizza. Lunch 19.50 euro, after 18:00 and Sunday 25.50 euro. Via del Teatro Pace 44.

Antica Trattoria Pallotta, this restaurant, one of my favorites in Rome, opened in 1820 and since then, its traditional recipes, great pizza and an internal garden, make it the right place for a pleasant dinner. Piazzale Ponte Milvio 23.

Ristorante Grotte di Livia, this restaurant offers its clients succulent typical dishes, and also a peculiarity as its own name suggests, Le Grotte, the Grottos, small natural caves where you can enjoy dinner in a more intimate setting. A special place for me. Piazza Saxa Rubra 9 (20 min from downtown Rome).

By the way, if you wonder if Livia is the owner's name, it is not. Livia Drusilla was the wife of the Roman emperor Augustus, she owned a villa in the area, the ancient Villa of Livia, some archeological remains of which are still visible.

Eggs a new concept restaurant where the organic egg is king and is celebrated, enhancing traditional and innovative recipes from appetizers to desserts, in its gourmet and inviting menu. Via Natale del Grande 52 www.eggsroma.com
La Pergola, a luxurious 3-Michelin-starred restaurant for a very sophisticated clientele, elaborate dish presentations and a spectacular view of Rome. Located at the Rome Cavalieri Waldorf Astoria hotel, via Alberto Cadlolo 101.
Mercato Centrale not exactly a restaurant, but an indoor food market with a modern yet sophisticated setting, where you can also sit and enjoy a very large selection of finger foods, desserts and more. Always busy with lots of clientele, very nice environment. A must try when in Rome. Via Giolitti 36.

After all this eating what is better than a refreshing, artisanal, genuine, ice cream? Let's go to a delicious gelateria!
Gelateria Della Palma, 150 tempting flavors. Take your time to make the very important decision of... which flavors to choose! Via della Maddalena 19 (near the Pantheon). By the way, Champagne flavor is among my favorites.
Gelateria Alaska, in addition to many other flavors, they have my very favorite cremino ice-cream, a rich, super decadent white and milk chocolate fudge flavor, I dream about from the plane on my way to Italy. Via Villa Severini 30.
Old Bridge, gelateria known for its generous portions of ice cream, I challenge you not to let it drip! Viale dei Bastioni di Michelangelo 5 (close to the Vatican).

Breakfast in Rome? Yes, in a pastry shop! Maritozzo con panna, the most traditional Roman-style sweet brioche, with the half-open top filled with whipped cream, perfect with cappuccino or coffee. La bomba fritta (the fried bomb), a round Roman fried cake of soft dough covered with sugar filled with custard cream. If you think the "bomba" sounds just a tiny bit like a calorie...bomb, you can opt for the lighter version, "la ciambella" (the doughnut) same flavor, but without custard cream. Of course, in addition to these three Roman sweets for breakfast, in a bar or pasticceria you will also find croissants in many flavors and other goodies to start a new and sweet (very sweet) day. And, in case one croissant doesn't satiate you and you're the daring type, the XXL cornetto will definitely do it: a gigantic 4 pounds of sweetness for you.... all your family, relatives and friends. Made by reservation only. Pasticceria De Santis Santa Croce, Via Santa Croce in Gerusalemme 17.

What if you are in Rome and, after reading about granitas, ice creams with brioches and other Sicilian delicacies, you would like to try them, but Sicily is not on your travel plans? No problem, Mondo Arancina brings you authentic Sicily to Rome! A must try. Sample a little bit of everything, from their wide selection of delicious Sicilian arancini, to bread with panelle (ask for a slice of lemon to squeeze over the panelle). Mondo Arancina, Via Marcantonio Colonna 38. Since you are there, you cannot miss (I am sure you won't once you see it) Gelarmony, right next door, at number 34. Wide selection of delicious gelati, granite, with (or without) brioches, a many other typical Sicilian desserts. What about the sandwiches and pizza filled with the many unique flavors of the Antico Vinaio di Firenze that I told you about a few pages ago? If going to Florence is not in your plans, but wanted to try its famous panini, no worries, since November 2021 it also has a location in Rome with special pizza/panini dedicated to this city (panino alla carbonara to name one). All'Antico Vinaio, Piazza della Maddalena 3.

On a cold or rainy day, or even if it is not cold or raining and not even very hot, but you'd rather stay indoors for a walk or to go shopping, have a bite to eat, a really nice place to do it is at Termini station, Rome's main train station. From the ground floor, going up the escalator to the upper floor there are eateries and gourmet restaurants, while going downstairs towards the subway you will find many stores of various kinds and have fun doing some shopping. Termini Station, via Giovanni Giolitti 40 (very close to Mercato Centrale at number 36).

So much to see, eat and do in Rome! Of course, in Rome as in other cities, when you are out exploring the culinary scene, when you see something new that catches your eyes and intrigues you, pause for a moment and check it out. It might be something you have never seen before, something that is only available in that city, so be curious and give it a try. A vacation is also this, the fun of discovering that "something" that YOU have captured (also capture it with your camera as you are happily savoring it, it will be a great memory to take home with you and continue to relish that moment). Have you ever heard a friend returning from a vacation saying something like "I was in such and such place, I saw this and that ..." then they pause for a moment, and excitedly say, "and the food ... oh the food! It was so delicious! I ate this and I ate that ... it was so amazing, if you go there, you REALLY must try it! "
 Food is such an important part of our vacations. Sometimes the new flavors we discover and enjoy can really touch our emotions down to our very being. I have traveled a lot and have seen many wonderful places and sceneries, and still, when I think of some places, I can also remember that delicious dish or dessert I tasted years ago during a vacation. I still remember it and I can talk about it with the same joy I felt years ago when I tried it.
As I said at the beginning of this chapter, food is a serious matter, especially if it is ... seriously delicious food!

A few more words...

We have reached the end of this book, it has been quite a journey (speaking of travel) for me to write it and take you to many corners of this "Bel Paese" this Beautiful Country, as it is called. It also gave me the opportunity to rekindle memories of places I had previously visited, but would love to return to, (and taste some delicious dishes again). Italy is much more than what I have described in these pages, there are many other beautiful places worth visiting.

Matera, for example, in the Basilicata region. This ancient town carved into the rock is one of the oldest inhabited settlements in human history. Its old districts, called Sassi, a series of caves carved into the limestone, make this town so unique as to be a Unesco World Heritage Site. The view of Matera seen approaching it from afar is truly fascinating and surreal at the same time. Strolling through the alleys of this quaint old town, you can find a restaurant with typical local dishes, a dessert with one of the most creative and delicious flavors to indulge in. Ristorante Soul Kitchen, an English name with an Italian heart for a heart-warming (or soul-warming I should say) Italian comfort food.
Civita di Bagnoregio, a tiny village perched on a promontory, about 120 km (75 miles) north of Rome. It is called "the dying town" because only 11 people live there, but on the contrary, Civita is still as quaint and charming as ever. It takes you back in time. Reachable on foot via a 1-km bridge (5-euro toll) uphill, or by shuttle (for a fee), it resembles the imaginary villages described in fairy tales, the ones that begin with "Once upon a time...". Every year thousands of people visit this fascinating village nestled in the Lazio countryside.
Le Marche, a region bordering Tuscany, has valleys, long coastlines and pretty towns like its more famous neighbor, Tuscany. Le Marche is the capital of luxury shoemakers (being Italy boot-shaped, this is appropriate, actually... fitting!). Brands like Prada have their precious Made in Italy footwear made there. Not to be missed are charming towns such as Pesaro, Urbino, Fabriano, or Fermo, with their history, art, quaint streets, the lovely village of Castelfidardo, cradle of the accordion instrument and its interesting museum, all in Le Marche.

See, I am starting to describe places again! Just as I said, there is much more to Italy than what I have described. To discover it to the fullest, also spending some time interacting with a local tour guide showing you other interesting aspects of a place besides the historical sites, to experience Italy in its many facets, would make your vacation even more fulfilling. Of course, for a variety of reasons, this is not always possible. Through the pages of this book, we have traveled together around Italy and shown you places you may not have known about, but which may now be part of your itinerary for your long-awaited trip to Italy. I shared side stories and trivia about some of the places we "visited", and also some of the fun things and activities you can do in Italy, how to get there and how to travel the length and breadth of this beautiful country. We saw many cities, landscapes, dreamy places, luxury hotels and budget friendly options, and of course, we talked about a delicious topic, food, the seriously good matter! Actually, all of the above is a seriously good, fun matter!

So, what makes a vacation a dream vacation? The combination of our desires and expectations coming true, to live, experience what we have dreamed and imagined, and sometimes what we live exceed even our dreams and what we have imagined! These are unforgettable moments that we will carry with us forever, in a special place in our memory, accompanied by a big smile every time we think about it. While you're making your Italian discoveries, do as the ancient Romans said and did: carpe diem, seize the moment! Take the time to savor that moment, wherever you are and whatever catches your curiosity. Of course, preparation and planning are also essential. Set aside some time to look at a map to decide how you want to create your vacation, what you would like to see, whether it is your first trip to Italy or your tenth, seeing just a few major cities as you travel across the country, or instead touring an entire region, (or perhaps two nearby) visiting the cities and landscapes, mountain, lake or sea, of that region. In short, the possibilities are endless.

Organize your personalized tour leaving some time free for the "extras" from your planned itinerary. When you arrive, don't rush, let yourself be surprised by the small or big unexpected "extras" that you will encounter during your holiday and that deserve a short "detour" for a little while, (a place, a street, a shopping spree, an impromptu boat ride, an unplanned dance night etc.), indulge, make time for the special extra that you find, soak up the atmosphere. After all, this is Your Dream Vacation To Italy, so embrace your dreams, keep dreaming until that moment, then and there, when you will finally live them!

After all this writing, I may need a vacation, and I have an idea of which country I want to go to, chances are it is the same as yours. See you there!
If you would like to leave a comment, we would love to hear from you.
The email address is: yourdreamvacationtoitaly@yahoo.com

Dream, plan and.. carpe diem!
Arrivederci e buon viaggio.

Travel notes: have fun writing what you would like to see and do in Italy, si... what you WILL see and do in Italy!